The Complete Guide to Politics for Black Preachers©

"But you should read it, too"

The Prequel

By: R. L. Dungy

The Complete Guide to Politics for Black Preachers © 2014
Raymond Dungy

FenceTalk Publishing © 2014

FenceTalk Publishing, Inc.
P.O. Box 70011
Mobile, AL 36670

ISBN-13: **978-1500347666**
ISBN-10: **1500347663**

Cover art and design © 2014 FenceTalk Publishing

Printed in the United States of America

In loving memory of my late parents Mr. and Mrs. E. R. Dungy; and to the freedom loving people, not just in America but all around the world.

"The tree of liberty must be refreshed from time to time with the blood of patriots and tyrants."

- Thomas Jefferson

Table of Contents

The Prequel

I finished writing "The Complete Guide to Politics for Black Preachers "...but you should read it too," in February of 2011.   At that time, I believe the good Lord would provide the funds to self-publish the book in plenty of time for it to have some bearing on the 2011 elections in November that year.   When that didn't happen, I was disappointed in God, and the outcome of the elections.   I reminded myself, as I often do, that God is much greater, bigger, loving, and smarter than I.   I comforted and calmed myself down by believing that God is up to something big. He always is.   Besides, the outcomes of the elections were more divine providence than voter count.   The third chapter of Isaiah bares this out.

I remember the look on Obama's face after he was announced the winner.   No one was more surprised than he.

It wasn't a look of joy, but shear shock and surprise that he managed to fool the American people a second time.   You see, there's no joy in being president of the United States for an ungrateful narcissist like Barak Hussein Obama. It's beneath him.   I am sure when he is around water the Secret Service dresses him in all kinds of flotation devices.   Being president, though shameful for him, is a necessary evil.   He's had his eye on that Mahdi gig for a while now.   Which explains his Cairo speech and all the other overtures and bone headed deals with terrorist states like Iran.   These are campaign moves made toward impressing the Jihadist electorate. He thinks he has a shot.   Iran's former president (dictator) Mahmoud Ahmadinejad, has been running a good terrorist campaign himself.   Having Ben Laden killed, hurt Obama's chances of getting the Al-Qaeda vote.   Which is why he tried to squirm out of having it done for three months after finding out his Pakistani whereabouts. The Hezbullah vote may still be in play.   We suspect he's been making overtures to them.   The American press is conflicted about who to support, President (dictator) Barak Obama, of the United States or Mahmoud.   Both are equally diabolical.

It's hard to believe more than 20% of American voters wanted anything more to do with Barak Obama.   In his first term, time and time again he proved himself to be incompetent, frightful, unconcerned, and an uninspiring Manchurian child in a big man's suit.   Even from a Black voter's perspective, what was there to want more of?   He had proven himself to be unconcerned and couldn't care less about Black people.   I know we are gluttons for punishment when it comes to Democrats, but this cat takes the cake, bakes the cake, and eats the cake when it comes to hurting us.   The gay marriage fiascos frighten most Blacks as well.   So if Black people had no reason to vote for him except out of foolish racial pride, what would the rest of America want with him? He had put a hurting on them too.   All that was left was Obama's symbiotic twins, the leftist, and the whack job computer geeks in bath robes, the anarchist, crazy liberals and the Twelvers.   They all hate America more than he.   Simply put, they hate God since he is the creator of all that's good and wonderful.   In short, my book wouldn't have had any effect on the outcome of the election.

---

*Note: **Barak Obama, was born in the African Nation of Kenya, attended Madrassa (Muslim school) in Indonesia and in large part was raised in Hawaii by his White grandparents, then mis-educated at Harvard. Therefore, by race hustler standards, he has no understanding or connection to Black people. Like a lot of actual Africans, he has no respect for American Blacks. They see us as nothing but whiners and complainers so hung up on racial self-pity, that we don't know how good we got it. They believe never has so little been down with so much. They see us as a mongrel race of people and themselves as "original" Black people. So it begs the uselessness of the African American tag. Even people living in huts and jungles with very little food to eat, look down their noses at us. Back in the early 20th century we mistakenly cast our lot with our former slavemasters the Democratic Party and the Civil Rights Movement.   Later came the race hustlers and poverty pimps.   All have been thorns in our side the knife in our backs, and the bane of our*** *existence ever since. Like most White Americans and other ethnic groups, they have become a bit tired of the whole: woe is me because of racism. Nobody gave them anything either. They quietly say they had to work hard for everything they have, and rightly so. The truth is the overwhelming majority of Black people punch a time clock five or more times a week and ask no one for nothing. It's the civil rights cabal that moans and groans supposedly on our behalf, but it's the Democrat party that's behind it. It's all done to get White people to feel guilty and vote against their best interest. So they brand us Black folks as poor, pitiful, hopeless people to make others feel guilty that it's somehow their fault. They make sure this "poor put upon" status stays with us. It makes White people jump through hoops to prove they're not racist and us on edge to make sure we show up to vote. I want the Hispanic community, to be mistrustful of the people the news media and Democrats appoint as their leaders. Run from them. Think for your individual selves. You better believe these self-appointed so-called leaders will sell you out at every turn. Before you know it, the Democrats will see you and treat you as their personal property the same way they do us Black folks. Then again, maybe selling out their people is unique to Black poverty pimps and race hustlers.*

So then with ego tattled, waiting for God's next move, knowing He's always up to something big, and after nearly two years of inward debate over who to get to write the forward to the book, who for eternity links their name to mine and suffer the blow back and persecution I might. I know nobody I dislike that much…maybe my youngest grandson…just kidding. He's only five and not half the monster he makes you think he is. I quietly delight in my son's come uppens everytime he calls to complain about the latest mischief. In the middle of all this inner debate, I realized that I hadn't even written an introduction to the book. So in October of 2013 I sat down to pen no more than seven lines and call it a day. Once I started the small chore, I kept writing and writing. Before I knew it I was up pass two in the morning for three months writing my seven line introduction. Afterwards, I realized that much of what I had written was what I wanted to put in the book, but, could never find the proper flow or place to put it. God, I believed, wanted me to write what he wanted me to. So with ego tattered I acquiesced. It's a hard thing to admit you're not that smart anyway and that your talent is on loan from God. So we leave it all on the field. When the fat lady sings and we retire to heavens locker room we are empty. We play the whole sixty minutes at that position God gave each of us. Henceforth there is a crown waiting for us. Because we gave all God gave us. All He put in us we give to the people. There is no knowledge in the grave. We hold no good thing from them. I thought writing this Prequel: in for a penny might as well be in for a pound. Hardly any of us escapes its scrutiny. I pray we all heed its warnings.

When I saw how long winded my introduction had become, I thought to myself….readers are going to say this dude loves to hear himself write, or this has to be the longest introduction to a book since Genesis. After counting the words and pages, I realized I had enough material for a pamphlet or booklet and most of the material is not directly covered in the original book.   So in the tradition of Star Wars prequel salesmanship, I offer you the prequel to my book "The Complete Guide to Politics for The Black Preacher, but you should read it too."   It may be small but it's got some big and impactful stuff in it.   So read it and pass it on to a liberal family member, friend, professor or preacher.   It will change their nutty and destructive belief system.   You don't have to "argue with idiots."   Just hand them this book and walk away. It will be hard even for a liberal to argue with an inanimate object; even though it speaks to their idiot beliefs.   So then they are resigned to read it.   Every junior high school student, as well as every high school, and college student every low – information voter, and everyone in the world should buy and read a copy of this book. America and the world lay in the balance. The leader of the free world hates the free world. Knowledge is power.   Make it happen.   Pass it on.

Introduction

In this book, I endeavor to explain politics; it's participants (how they operate) its functions, goals, allies, methods, plots, schemes, dangers, history and end-game, both to the political astute, and the politically clueless. Thanks to a godless propagandist news media, a heathenish entertainment industry, a near worthless education system, and a know nothing clergy, we are awashed in uninformed clueless voters. These are easily manipulated again and again into voting against their best interest.   They cast their lots with evil maniacal politicians, who they foolishly believe operate in their best interest.

Thanks to all of the before-mentioned; America has no shortage of ignorant and idiotic voters.   Their total and complete knowledge of politics starts and ends with find the

"D" for Democrat and pull the level or punch the corresponding chad and their civic duty is finished until next time.   Then they slink back into "American Idol" and "The Kardashians" or whatever mind numbing distraction that occupies their time.   If they tell you they give thought, or use any other criteria for their mindless voting decision, they lie. They're post hoc folly is mind blowing.   These are guided by nothing more than an emotional assessment that Democrats care about them and their plight.

In writing this book, I've employed line upon line; precept upon precept; here a little there a little, to convince the most ardent Democrat party supporter that nothing could be further from the truth.   Democrats are nothing more than dirty rotten lowdown rat fink bastards, whose end-game is to enslave us all.   Remember, Democrats were the original and only slave-owners in our nation's history.   They fought a bloody civil war to retain the right to keep Black people as chattel and personal property.   The Republican Party was started in the mid 1850's to stop slavery. Since their progenitor Andrew Jackson, who owned several hundred slaves, to this day, nothing animates them more than returning to this they're golden age.   This time their whipping boards, shackles and plantations are aimed at America as a whole.   They dream of a day of Stalinist styled forced labor camps for all Americans outside of their ruling class sphere.   Regardless of race, color, creed, economic status, religion, gender and party affiliation under Democrats' just as Uncle Joe (Stalin) did, wants to enslave you.

Their lust for total and complete control over the lives of Americans, knows no bounds, nor moral constraints.   These are scruples free.   They dream about this final solution, their energy and every conscience moment, even when they sleep is dedicated to its design and implementation. Their Trojan horse promised of a utopian society will only defecate a dystopian one. If we don't wake up and listen to the voices crying in the wilderness, we will awake to find ourselves up to our eyeballs in marxist doodoo. We can't take the fall back position and say any Democrat mayor, governor, congressman, senator nor dog catcher is different. They are all one in the same: predators.

Democrats Robin Hood, rant and riff of taking from the rich and giving to the poor to accomplish this utopian pipe dream has the same mythological value the story does. Still, they've gotten plenty of mileage out of it. More than any of his other attributes Robin Hood, was a thief. In my world of blue skies, white clouds and not many pies flying around, thieves don't risk life, limb nor incarceration only to give their spoils away. In their robbery of the rich and the middle class (i.e., anyone with a job) through higher taxes in order to pay for social programs and utopia, they keep upwards of 75% of the spoils for themselves and their political allies.

While they rob others of money, they rob the poor of self-esteem, self-determination, and self-effort. Far too many nestle into the trap of a social safety net of government handouts and dependency. Then their communities become a breeding ground for most of our social ills. Like bacteria geminates in a petre dish, so does out of wedlock births, fatherless children, crime, drug abuse and incarceration. All aberrant behavior grows in this environment. Lyndon Johnson's, "Great Society" (1965) and Franklin Roosevelt's, "New Deal" (1933-1938) has been nothing but a raw deal for hundreds of thousands of Americans. Over the years these utopians lies have destroyed the lives of untold Americans, especially those in the Black community.   This was always the design of these so-called poverty programs by these Democratic presidents to destroy the Black community. Maybe not so much with Lyndon Johnson, but certainly with Roosevelt.   Yet, both utopian plans have been equally devastating to the Black community.   When these atrocities happen to Black folk, Democrats and their friends in the liberal news media blame Republicans.   It's Republicans who have been trying to save Black people from Democrats since slavery.

Like Jesus' gospels this is a love letter first to the Black preachers and their congregations, then to America at large then to the world.   Better than half of Black Americans attend church on a weekly basis. Of these, the overwhelming majority get their political marching orders from their pastor. Ninety-plus percent of the time these instructions are find the "D" and vote Democrat.   No thought or concern is given to their political stances or individual moral beliefs.   Most Black pastors give this recommendation out of tradition and shear ignorance.

It has been this way since the advent of the civil rights movements and with the election of avowed racist Democrat president Woodrow Wilson, in 1915.   It was the Black vote that put him over the top.   Once in office he started to fire as many Blacks working in the government as possible. All he didn't fire, he segregated away from the White workers. Before this he ran campaigns to kick Blacks who attended his beloved alma mater Princeton, out.   He played NAACP president WEB Dubois, for a fool who supported him for president. Up until then, Blacks had supported Republican candidates.   When asked about what he had been doing to Black people, Wilson said, "they knew what I was before they voted for me".   The news media loves to talk about the oddly named "Saturday Night Massacre" on October 20, 1973. Then Republican President Richard Nixon, fired one special prosecutor.   Wilson, fired hundreds of Blacks from civil service jobs held by them for years.   The media is not interested in telling about this "Saturday Night Massacre".

Even so, election after election, they regurgitate this same old non-sense that Democrats represent the best interest of Black folks.   Nothing can be further from the truth.   Most Black preachers don't want to get in trouble with the Democrats, and their congregations by bucking this tradition. Sadly, some are woefully ignorant of the truth. Höerbiger's ice theory rings truer. Even sadder, some are willfully ignorant of the truth.   Their hear no evil, see no evil, ostrich posture protects them from knowing, thus, preventing them from spouting the truth.   Yet, the truth is the only thing that makes us free.

An acquaintance once told me, there is another kind of Black preacher in the political realm who is paid off to support a certain Democrat candidate.   He told me how he and others use to carry around so-called "walk-around" or "bag money" to bribe Black preachers around the state of Arkansas, for supporting former senator David Pryor, and other Democrats. Seriously, would anybody be surprised to find out that this kind of graft and corruption is taking place throughout the United States, especially where large Black populations reside.   I was told by another friend, more politically astute than I, with a nod from the right Black preacher in a given voting district a politician can get the Black clergy support, thus, the Black vote.   This has been a tried true and tested route to political victory for Democrats.

I have watched Barak Obama, pay-off certain Black preachers with twiddle your thumbs meaningless appointments to advisory councils.   Others are given grant moneys not to preach against Obama's abominable gay marriage, and baby killing agenda.   Sadly, most Black preachers were already silent on both issues, for fear of offending members of their congregation and the Democrat Party.   What about offending God?

Some Black preachers have gone as far as denying the Lordship of Jesus Christ, in order to fit into Barak Obama's, self-dietfying perceptions.   He sees himself as Messiah. That's why he refuses to mention God in his speeches. Maybe T. D. Jakes, should remember this next time he defends Obama's Christianity and questions George Bush's. There's not one shred of evidence that Obama is a Christian, other than his reluctance to say he is.   Not one raisin fruit exist.   The Bible says you will know a tree by the fruit it bares.   There are apple orchards and garden groves of evidence that he is a forerunner to the Anti-Christ.   In the same way John the Baptist, was a forerunner to Jesus Christ.

It is something supernaturally demonic or omenish about him.   In the way he gets his political way, and how people invest full faith and credit that he is Messiah.   Especially those Black people who get red faced mad when ever somebody says anything negative about him.   Christians should have no other gods before God.   Outside of his beautiful wife and his button cute daughters, there's nothing good to say about him.   You can say what you want to about Messiah Jesus Christ, but watch your mouth when it comes to messiah Barak Obama.   For some his cult of personality is that demanding.   It's one thing for non-church going Blacks to think of him as Messiah, it's another for church going ones to shout Hosanna Bar-Damien.   To put ones skin color above right and wrong or God is idolatrous and dangerous.   I speak as Joash, Gideon's father: "If Baal is all that let him defend himself." NDV (New Dungy Version).   It's time to throw down altars erected to politicians, especially Obama.

Note: These statements are not intended to be primo monkey spank porn for the "rapture" and "world coming to an end" crowd.   These beat off at any and every hint of Anti-Christ sightings or apocalyptic nuances. Throughout history the silly-wing of Christianity sees the Anti-Christ everywhere, especially since Scoffield and his minions ranted on a pre-trib rapture back in the early part of the 20th century.   These see the Anti-Christ in more places than Elvis fans see him.   We need to be real about the here and now.   When it comes to these people anything about Y2K or any prophesy book published you might as well give it the Playboy, or Hustler brand. People like Hal Lindsey, is their Larry Flint.   All of Christendom should stop seeing some future event as an excuse to sit on their hands and let the rest of America go to hell.   The silly-wing of Christianity would rather see an openly wicked and dangerous person who's hostile to every value America holds true in the White House, before supporting someone who didn't meet all of their idolatrous needs of perfection in a man and his orthodoxy.   Maybe they considered him the Anti-Christ.   On the subject of prophesy their flights of crazy knows no bounds.   They may have reasoned that Obama, couldn't be the Anti-Christ because he's openly evil; ergo Mick Romney, could be because he's too polished and slick looking. Still, family wise, church wise, business wise, charity wise, Governor Romney, has led an almost perfect and honorable life.   I much rather have a non-professing Christian, who does everything right as a friend, than a professing one that does everything wrong.   A lot of honorable men would be happy to untie Mick Romney's shoes.   But, the evangelical elites found a way to look even further down their puritan noses at him last election. Naturally, his way of life offends the hell out of the average Democrat voter.   They tend toward hating virtues like truth and honor. What they envision is someone taking all of Romney's money and giving it to them. Mick Romney's decency as a human being should have counted for something amongst more evangelical voters. The silly wingers believe that death, destruction, and calamity will usher in the advent of Jesus Christ. The Shia Muslims believe the same will bring the12th Iman out of hiding. That's why they want a nuclear bomb. Maybe the two should work together. While I didn't vote for Governor Romney, in the Republican primary election, I was at the door, at the open, to vote for him in the general. At that point, I was chomping at the bit to vote for Elmer Fudd, and his running mate Daffy Duck, if it meant getting rid of the abominable desolate sitting in the White House now. Sadly, the evangelical elites are much more interested in presenting a purest pretend than saving America.   Somehow they've gotten it in their heads that they are not suppose to participate in politics. They have drunken the Jonestown java, on this point. Eddie B, warned that "all evil need to triumph is good men do nothing." And that's what most of Christendom has gotten proficient at doing, nothing. May God have mercy on our souls. It's all beneath them to make bother. But these need to know, while they are not "of" this world, they are still "in" this world and subject to the stench of its rot. The cultural decay takes place only because they won't use the salt God gave them to not only sweeten and season the world but to preserve it. Christians have the kingdom keys to drive America out of the ditch Obama and the Democrats are obsessed with keeping us in. The silly-wingers labor under a Scoffieldian prescience that tells them that God will rapture them out of here when things get bad and right before the anti-christ makes his debut, so then they are lulled into pastures of ease, sitting on the dock of the bay watching the world roll away with passports in pocket, waiting departure. Heavenly bound, but no earthly good. Forget the "Great Commission" these await the "Great Escape". They sit gazing up at the sky waiting on the return of Jesus Christ, but, the anti-christ shows up instead. Only because they're leisure allowed the apostasy to take place that would usher in the advent of the Anti-Christ. Their falling away caused the Holy Spirit, to be taken out, therefore allowing that "Wicked" to be revealed. Twice in the Bible it says he (the Anti-Christ) will make war with the saints. How does this happen if we are in Heaven? Does that "Wicked" come into Heaven and offer us a beat down. Scoffield said we want be here. Then how is it he prevails *against the saints.   He got kicked out of Heaven.   But Scoffield and his disciples say we won't be here.   Clearly, it's a lie and a trick of the devil to lull us into this Lunesta styled sleep in which we have been in for all these years. Christians have been lulled into a lackadaisical paralyzed state. So many have been fooled into believing the pretrib rapture lie. The old and new testament talks about a fight where the Anti-Christ is going to kick the crap out of us. He will wear Christians out.   While we are here on earth. Reading the 24th chapter of Matthew, I discovered that war, pestilence and death are already in full blown mode all around the world, as it is right now. The saints are in full retreat running into mountains leaving their worldly possessions behind.   Pregnant women praying its day when they make their way out of Dodge.   If we follow the definite article "then" in the 24th chapter; chronologically we find that apocalyptic events line up with a post tribulation rapture.   From verses 3 through 29 all hell breaks loose.   Yet, as early as the 15th verse the Anti-Christ has found the temple of the Lord to be nice diggs and measuring for curtains (NDV).   It isn't until the 30th verse that a sign of Jesus appears in the heavens. Even then I am not sure when he actually intercedes in what's happening here on earth.   Moreover, no talk of rapture occurs until the 40th verse.   I listen to all of the pre-and mid trib proponents, where they take you out to the Orion belt and back to explain their theories.   Me, I just read the Bible. Christians, silly ones, lazy ones, and other ones, need to offer a country who now readily accepts the spirit of Anti-Christ that already is in the world a choice to choose.   We need to offer them Jesus Christ.*

If the rapture is pending evangelism becomes even more of an imperative. The thing that I have learned in my sixteen years of street evangelism is that people are more willing to accept Jesus Christ as Lord and Savior, than not. Truly the harvest is plenteous but the laborers are few. When Jesus is presented in a loving non-judgmental way sinners are happy to receive Him. It's hard to turn away or reject the Man who died for you and your sins. The homosexual needs someone to tell and show them the love of Jesus Christ. They need to know Jesus wants to save them and love them right out of their bondish. It may not happen overnight but Jesus wants to and will deliver them. So it goes for every lost soul. No judgments need to be made, just love shown. It's time to dismount the high horse and get down in the muck and mire with these precious people. Let the Holy Spirit be your guide as to when, and where, and how. As Christians, we need to make our presence known in every aspect of American life. The highways and byways as well as up and down and throughout politics. If you don't like a slate of candidates, find your own. There is no rapture that's going to snatch, harpoon nor take us out of here when things get really bad. I wish it was. So let's make America and the world the best place on earth to live. God gave us the power to do that. We are the salt of the world.

Those Black preachers who speak out against Obama's evil agenda, lives and families are threatened by his minions.

Creflo Dollar, was verbally crucified by members of the Congressional Black Caucus, for his stance against gay marriage.

Some Black pastor's scapegoat and pussy-out by saying they don't preach politics. I thought murder and homosexuality were first affronts to God and not decided by the dictates of man, especially, evil politicians. I also thought, "thou shalt not kill," and "man should not lie with man" were God's purview and not subject to the whims of evil politicians. These malcontents put it under the heading of political speech, so they can threaten preachers, rabbis and priest with a tax exempt status recall if they preach against them. This ain't politics. This is the en-errant word of God.

Have we forgotten what God did to a place called Sodom and Gomorrah? How he rained down fire and brimstone and burned those cities to ashes because of their sexual perversion. What makes us believe he won't do the same thing to a place called United and States? Just like fire and brimstone burned down these wretched cities our families are being burned down with divorce, our children are being burned away with illicit sex and drugs. Our economy is being burned down with intentional government mismanagement along with our way of life. Our health-care system is being burned down with Obamacare. Our babies, thus our future is being burned away with abortion mills. One out of four crotches in America are burning with some kind of sexually transmitted disease. Our inner cities are being burned down with crime, despair, drugs and fatherlessness. Our schools are being burned down with the woes of the overall culture. Women's lib, alternative and unrepentant life styles, social programs, the welfare state, greed, godless politicians…yet, more than all of these a prayerless, powerless, silent pulpit are to blame.   Righteousness exalts a nation but sin is a reproach to any nation. A curse does not come without a cause.

To pile upon these maladies, our coastal cities are being blown away or drown in flood waters due to hurricanes.   Our inner townships (it's not just trailer parks anymore) are being shredded and ripped apart by tornadoes.   The death and property damage tolls escalate with each rain drop.   Arctic snow storms and drifts, drought, heatwaves, river floods, and forest fires affect the rest.   Who knows what ten plus rector scale earthquakes are lurking beneath or pathogens.   Sin not global warming is the culprit. (Genesis 6th chapter). We have some real "Day of the Lord" stuff going on here.   The wrath of God is upon us and the silent song from the pulpits around America plays on. God is slowly lifting His hand of protection from us.

The Black pulpits across America need to get back to the mandate of God, and rid itself from this destructive relationship it has had with the godless Democratic party. This book, I believe, will go a long way toward that turnabout by answering all questions to all of politics.   This truth will get the so-called Black pulpits and preachers and Black folk free of the Democratic party, thus, its demons. Now we no longer fight with them, we fight against them. We have warmed by the enemy's fire long enough.

They and their adjuncts (news media, ACLU, Hollywood) have tried to rid this nation of every vestige of God they could from the public arena.   But, try as they do, there is no separating church and state.   What is wrong in sermons on Sunday is wrong in politics Sunday through Sunday.   You can't leave God in the car when you go in to vote.   No more than you can leave him out of the equation when you die. He sees the God-hating politicians you knowingly vote for and hold you responsible for the evil actions they take while in office.   Everytime they vote to increase funding for more abortions with taxpayer money, so do you. What is wrong for a Christian to do is equally wrong for an unbeliever to do.   It rains on the just and the unjust. One thing for sure, "every knee shall bow and every tongue will confess that Jesus is Lord."   Even Barak Obama, and his messianic delusions.   So will T. D. Jakes, since he's ambivalent about who Jesus is.   He will find out just who Jesus is.   So will world renowned evangelist and Democrat Billy Graham.   We all should pray they don't find out the hard way.   We pray they and all the rest will hear "well done" instead of "depart from me".   Just like the traffic signs and the laws of gravity apply to everyone so does God's laws of moral conduct.   From Adam and Eve, till now, God's statutes on ethical behavior remain the same.   He is God and He changes not.

When you fix the "Black" pulpit you fix a lot of what's wrong in the Black community, by extension America.   It's a wag the dog principle that God will get behind.   All the woes in the Black community will precipitously drop when we turn from the Democratic party (we owe them nothing), and the word of God is preached without favor compromised and looking over one's shoulder.   The answers to all of America's problems rest in a return to God, not government.   Especially some marxist street thug from Chicago.   I am sorry "community organizer" trained in the Alinsky tradition.

The Black Voter

In far too many Black people, there lies an inability or willingness to admit fault, or say I'm sorry. More than other ethos it's a blind side we can't see. Maybe it's all the years of Democrats and the race hustlers telling us nothing is our fault or responsibility. Maybe it derives from DNA or some other stimuli. Nevertheless, the inability not to be able to admit to one's faults is to stay trapped inside a cage with an open door. When content of character ceases to carry the day then ones color become its umpire. Now every defense of aberrant behavior gets dumped in the skin color file and stamped innocent or racism is our albatross. Certainly, the Black kid who robbed the liquor store five times wasn't at fault. The outside forces of racism were clearly to blame. All of the store's camera footage proves it.   So then the little thug is given an apology and another rip at the liquor store.   To avoid admitting fault or saying I am sorry, Black people will grab at any lie or elusion and hold on for dear life. So it is with our voting for Democrats.   At the most Black voters might secretly, for a fleeting moment, late at night, when no one is around, ever so quietly admit to themselves: Democrats have not been good for us.   Openly, they will clutch to the lie as if their lives depend on it.   When you argue politics with them, you're not necessarily arguing with their emotions or their total lack of evidence to prove any of their assertions.   No, you are arguing with their total need to be right regardless of the reality and truth presented them.   They can't admit that they've been wrong, so the little birdie doesn't escape its open cage.   It's a lot better than becoming free and taking flight. Almost universally, Blacks can't phantom the idea that Democrats have made fools of them   or "played" them for all these years and they wasn't smart enough to recognize it. Fool me once, shame on you. Fool me a million times after that then…? To say I am sorry or I am wrong is a betrayal of fool's pride that goeth before the fall.

Several categories of Black voters have evolved over the years. One such Black voter is the "do nothing phony." These need to feel that they care or at least have others think that they do.   They want others to believe that they care about less fortunate Black folks without doing a damn thing.   They sacrifice no time nor treasure.   In lieu of lifting a finger, they wrap themselves in the Democrat party flag and it absorbs them of any fiduciary to their Black brethren. They vote for any Democrat because "they care" is the care without caring ribbon they darn to the rest of us.   They're given Mother

Theresa, size brownie points by other couldn't careless Black folks. They relax themselves into a cushiony proud posture of "keeping it real" with no dirt under their fingernails. After all, they did all they needed to do and gave all they needed to give at the polling place.

There's that category Black voter who election after election takes one more stab with blind faith and tradition. Maybe this time things will change for the better. Maybe this time they will do what they say they're going to do. Then they never do. They never will. The "maybe this time" Black voter lacks Albert Einstein's perspective and definition on insanity.

Then comes the "something for nothing" Black voter, they believe the universe owes them something and the Democrats are going to make doggone sure it pays up. Even if its little green men from Mars, they need to fork over some space money too. Even God Himself is not exempt from a Democrat party shakedown on behalf of its patrons, the sad sacks believe. Strangely, if you dare ask them what they owe, proudly they will tell you: they don't owe nobody a damn thing. It's all these years of Democrat breeding at fault.

These don't touch the insanity of the "imbecile" Black voter. For these crackpots there is no truth, law or fact outside that told them by the Democrat party. If told the sky is purple with orange polka dots, they're faith in Democrat party propaganda and talking points is such they won't even look up to verify the lie. Nothing in them has the ability to say, that doesn't make sense. Nothing outside of Democrat lies ring true to them. These whack jobs like to think of themselves as highly intelligent, smart people. I am sure all of the research and case studies will prove they do.   These idiots are not savants.

While listening to a national radio talk show, the host after monumental effort and perseverance momentarily convinced an imbecile that Abraham Lincoln, and the Republicans, freed the slaves from Democrat slaveowners, who treated them like dirt.   The imbecile quipped that they (the slaveowners) must of knew what they were doing.   The host amazed at the imbecile's retort asked, what about Abraham Lincoln, freeing the slaves?   The diminished capacitate said "good for him."   What about good for us? There is no rationale that seeps they're psyche.   Also at their core, they are seething mad, angry, poor pathetic people that Democrats prey upon by feeding this anger.   Liars like Obama, tell them they have a right to be mad at everything. Obama says vote for me and I'll get even with those imaginary people stomping around in your head.   There may be daddy issues with these crazy people.   I'll check the case studies to find out.

The worst of the Black voter type is the "anarchist" or "radical".   These sick bastards love seeing the devastation released on the Black community by the Democrat party. They are tantalized by the daily body count on the local evening news of Black boys hunting each other down and killing one another like animals.   It's done with such frequency, accuracy, efficiency, and sport that it may wait Olympic Committee approval.   "The hunt the nigger and kill the nigger by other nigger's driveby-athon."   The radical or anarchist Black voter receives like pleasure when they see thirteen and fourteen year old Black girls pregnant. Some with their second child. There's a glee in their eyes and an orgasmic curl in their toes when they watch the anarchy that has besieged the inner city. All compliments of the Democrat party, race hustlers, and poverty pimps. The only time they feign anger at some Black guy being murdered is when some crazy White boy down in Florida, kills a Black youth in self defense. Killing is killing; dead is dead, regardless of who was killed or who did the killing. But, the hypocrites in the Black community don't see it this way. We all should be mad at the senseless death of any and every young person regardless of the cause. There should be no respecter of murdered or murderer. Sadly, but not surprisingly, the young man's unfortunate death served as a political opportunity for Barak Obama, the Obama-ites, the civil rights hypocrites, poverty pimps and race hustlers, in short, the usual suspects. The Democrat party cabal shamelessly all piled atop this boy's body. Even though none of them couldn't care less about this young man or his family they hopped their high horse and immediately started shouting injustice and racism. This was before any hard facts were known. Especially, since Florida, self-defense and gun laws are the most liberal in the country. My guess is, because of this, they have the lowest pro-rata robbery and murder rates in the country. But none of this could be taken into account when the cabal gets in gear to make its fraudulent charges of racism and injustice. Their golden opportunity awaits them; they hit the tri-fecta with this child's "timely" death. The civil rights movement needed the headlines, the Democrat party needed the angry Black voter registration drive, and Barak Obama, needed the distraction from his miserable stewardship of our nation. These grave robbers cut this boy's body up into three pieces. These animals have no shame, nor scruples.   The cabal's situational ethics and outrages are appalling enlight of the thousands of Black on Black murders taking place months prior and months since. Yet, not a peep is heard from them.   There's no gold in these hills.   These are good at pointing fingers, but never lifting one.   Black hypocrites walk around wearing T-shirts with Travon Martin's picture.   Where are the T-shirts of the tens of thousands of other young black boys and men gunned down?   Wasn't their lives important too?   No, their deaths didn't meet the requirements for racial self-pity and the Democrat cabal need to score political points.   Remember, Rahm Emanuel, said "A tragedy is a terrible thing to waste."

Nothing angers the Black anarchist more than the concept or the possibility of a successful Black person. These are called "sell-outs" and "Uncle Toms" by the radical Black anarchist.   Obama gets a pass.   These need the pictures of devastation in order to hide or excuse their total failure at life and as human beings.   Their entire purpose in life now, is to discourage as many young Blacks from pursuing their dreams, goals and aspirations in life.   They use all kind of name calling like "wannabes" to stop them from taking advantage of every educational opportunity in their early lives so that their later lives will not be successful and productive.   Misery loving company is not a cliché when it comes to these bozos.   They and the poverty pimps for years has leveled charges of Uncle Tom, and sell-out at every Black person trying to do something positive with their lives.   First of all, Uncle Tom, has nothing to do with what these idiots think it does.   Secondly, I sell these dirt bags out every chance I get.   Every time I pick up a golf club, I sell these Neanderthals out.   Every time I find myself with more than lint in my pocket, I sell these nothings out.   Every time I go to church, I sell these pathetic people out.   Every time I pronounce a word correctly, I sell these negativity vipers out. Every time I smile at a White person, I sell these disgusting people out.   Every time I make more than a "D" on a test paper or class grade, I sell these sub-humans out.   Every time I don't call myself an African American, I sell these assholes out.   Every moment I am not in handcuffs or in jail, I sell these bastards out.   Every second I spend alive and well, I sell out these loathsome nothings.   I refuse to live my life according to the desire or dictates of these animals. "Keeping it real" becomes so damn paralyzing and destructive. It's only a banner to hide all kinds of aberrant behavior behind.   I don't waste time trying to please people that don't matter to me or my goals, dreams, and aspirations. These clowns should have no shadow of turning in no Black person's life.

But these need the pictures of a Black community wasteland in order to hurl charges of racism at White people, especially those that might vote Republican. They need White people ate up with unnecessary guilt, and Black people falling in line and going along with every stupid thing they breed.   It gives them worth, nothing else does.

These whackos are so screwed up they call God a racist. One once ask me, how can a black cow eat green grass, then squirt white milk?   I gave him my short answer, I am glad the milk isn't black or green I said to the credent.   I am not even that fond of chocolate milk.   It wasn't my first time answering this stab at calling God Almighty a racist.   I usually go: the cow has three, four, five stomachs and yada yada.   There is no rock, pebble or grain of sand these assholes want kick over to find a morsel of racism to explain the utter uselessness of their existence.   It's sad to think of all those Black people who might be in hell or be in imaginary cages because they couldn't look within themselves and say I am the problem and repent.   Nothing is more liberating.   Take this to the bank, ninety nine percent of the time, it's the man in the mirror that's the problem and solution.

We have our "traditional" Black voter, grand-momma and grand-daddy voted Democrat.   So did momma and daddy. Chances are great- granddaddy and great-grand-momma voted Republican, before we made the devastating switch to start voting Democrat.   Cursed by their more immediate blood line, they can't or won't think out of the box.   They can't or won't entertain the idea that it might be unprofitable or regressive in voting for Democrats.   If you're this closed minded about politics, what other outside of the box million dollar ideas that you close yourself off to, because you know only one way of looking at the world.   To paraphrase Jesus, your traditions have cut you off from me and what I want to do with your life.   God wants to give us witty inventions and million dollar ideas.   Traditional thought patterns won't get you there.   I overheard some Black traditionalist say Black people have no business playing golf.   First chance I got, I went and looked into purchasing golf clubs.   Good thing Calvin Peete and Tiger Woods didn't think that way.   In order to fit into the narrow scope of "keeping it real" traditionalist keep it stupid and fail to look beyond the horizon and say: the skys the limit for where God wants to take me. My favorite verse of scriptures is Ephesians 3:20 "Now unto Him who can do exceeding abundantly above all we can ask or think according to the power working in me."   I know most Black church traditionalist hate this verse. But, it tells me no matter how big I dream, God is dreaming even bigger for me. I don't have to stay poor, Black, and die the way the Democrat party's cabal or starchamber wants me to. I can go way beyond their plots to stamp me out. God placed in me all the ability I need to get me where He wants to take me. The Latin word for education "educare" which means to bring up or out of us what's already in us. In other words, a great piano player is already one before even knowing what a piano is. All that's needed is the proper stimuli and opportunity. The thing is, I can't bring what's in me out of me if I am thinking inside the traditionalist box, comfortable amongst go nowhere friends. There is no greater liberation than to be free from the opinions of men, once you discover who you are in Jesus Christ. Pleasing Him becomes your focus. The fact of the matter is, He's already pleased with you. Everybody else simply becomes people you love and cherish, not whose opinions of you, matter.

Another category of Black voter is the "A" political ones. They typically don't hate God, Republicans and America. They go about their lives clueless and un-phased by the daily political squabbles. They watch it all out of the corner of their eye. At times, they can tell you who the president is. That's as far as their acriment goes. Who their governor, congressman and US senator are, is way above their pay grade to bother to know. Yet, whenever a Democrat is behind in the polls and on the verge of losing a race for whatever political office, either the local marxist media or the national news marxist find some innocent thing that may have happened with the Republican candidate, put the racist toe tag on it, and generate anger and voter registration drives. At the same time scaring off a lot of spineless White voters. So then the "A" political Black emotion's are manipulated to the point that they take time out of their busy schedules to register and vote for the Democrat, who more than ninety percent of the time is a hidden avowed racist.   Despite his or her skin color. So then the "A" political Black voter becomes a useful idiot like the rest.

Lastly, and least are those Black voters like myself. We don't drink the Democrat party's Jonestown cool-aid. We are roughly ten percent of the Black voting electorate. We are called Uncle Toms and sell outs.   But our moral compass helps us recognize scumbags when we see them.   We don't compromise on abortion, school prayer, homosexual's lifestyles and the welfare state. All are reprehensible. We realize the Democrat slave-master of the mid-1800's are the same today.   More than ever they see us as nothing more than personal chattel, and lust for the day when they can say it out loud and prostate us accordingly.   Legal or illegal immigration goes a long way toward replacing us as a voting block with new "Mexican niggers."   Their motives are not to increase their voters, it's to replace us as a voting block. Then they can finally tell us how they really feel about us. Even then, the brain-washing has been so intense for all these years, that they still might lose only a few Black votes.

We "ten percenters" believe first that homosexuality is an abomination in Gods eyes.   The welfare state is a deliberate destruction of the Black race via the Black family.   That every American student should have the right to pray before class and abortion is primarily geared toward the annihilation of the Black race by Democrats and their liberal White voters. Democrats have place 90% of Plan Parenthood abortion…

Note: Know this: White Democrats or liberals have an inordinate fear of Black people. Whether it's penis envy or some kind of rise of the planet of the apes scenario that rattles them. They find it necessary to support the openly stealthy annilations of the Black race through abortion and other means, such as the welfare state by the Democrat party. There is no sane reason to vote for Democrats. White liberals except their own loss of freedom via higher taxes and senseless regulations when it comes to voting for Democrats, as a cost of doing business. People who fear rats, roaches, spiders or snakes can't wait for somebody to show up and kill them. They hate even more the thought of being overrun by them. For a lot of White Democrat voters this is what allies them to the party. The segregation of the south is what kept White southerners loyal to the Democrat party, up until they figured out that Democrats were out to get them too. So they switched alliances and became the Republican South. Yet, White liberals have convinced themselves they are good people because they vote for the people who "care". All the time seeing Black people as nothing more than household critters or pest to be stomped out of existence. Human nature is you hate what you fear. Hate is never far behind fear. During the years prior to World War II, Adolf Hitler first made German Anglo-Saxons fear Jews rising above them socially and economically. Hitler and his Nazi party generated so much fear, then hate primarily for Jews that he didn't have to fire a shot to become Chancellor of Germany. Then he became "The Fuhrer." He threw around a lot of nordic and superior race gibberish and some evolution and monkey talk to dehumanize them. Now the planet of the ape's scenario became real in the head of the Germans. Once the German elites feared being overran by the primate Jews, Hitler was then free to order the extermination of the Jews with the German people's blessing. Fear is a powerful motivator.

...mills in and around Black communities, Democrat mayors and city councilman are the biggest obstacles to getting drugs and crime out of the Black community.   What's the why? Their attitude is, nigger you are going to vote for me no matter how I screw over you.   They have no incentive to do nothing but allow the rot to continue.   Those resources (police patrol) might be used to protect some other nationality whose votes we are not guaranteed.   The truth is Democrats have been trying to wipe us out since the Emancipation Proclamation.

Since Roe vs. Wade, almost every Democrat running for office especially in the eastern states and cities there has been a wink or a nod to White voters that they were going to do their part to annihilate the Black race.   They never say it out loud.   It's simply understood what the game plan will continue to be and that's to get rid of those, planet of the ape niggers. There is no other reason White liberals vote for Democrats.   By definition, course and stealthiness, liberals are Nazi bigots.

Voting Democrats

With each passing day it becomes more and more apparent, even unto the most ardent Democrat supporter that Democrat politicians are dirty rotten low-down fink rat bastards out to get us all. Obama's economy, Obama's foreign policy disasters, worse than these Obamacare notwithstanding, Democrats up and down the political food chain prove they are not to be trusted with the affairs of governing. Not even for city dump supervisor or its shop stewards. Sanitation workers can go on strike and leave your city in a stinky bind. So if a city dump supervisor or union leader wheels that much destructive power, imagine the damage a Democrat mayor, governor, congressman, senator, and president can cause. No matter the political office or station Democrats, will burn you.   It's a done deal, just a matter of how and when.   No American after a time of reflection can say they've never been burned by a Democrat office holder.   They have and will rob you blind.   Maybe it's safe to trust them with your dead pet rattlesnake, I wouldn't recommend it.

Very few neighborhoods in America can honestly say they've never been burned by a Democrat.   They cast a wide net of destruction regardless of their soaring mountain size rhetoric, nice smiles, electrifying oratory, vague innocuous promises, and designer suits and dresses. Once they are in office and its spoils and privileges avail, job one is to rape, rob and pillage their charge on behalf of their political machines, union bosses, and fat cat cronies.

Often, the negative effects of their stewardship isn't known or made manifest until they've left office.   Almost always a city, county or state is saddled with higher taxes and more unfunded liabilities and mandates.   What municipalities have in return for their sodomization is failing schools, higher budget deficits, crumbling infrastructure, higher crime rates, higher unemployment, and more people in need of public assistance.   So much for their vague innocuous promises. When you get in bed with the devil only bad things happen.

In much the same way the national marxist media walks behind Obama, with a giant pooper scooper, so does local media for local Democrats.   They cover it all up by blaming the voters for expecting too much, or on whatever Republican is standing nearby.   Their termite operandi is always the same. The local media paints the house with nice bright pretty colors, while Democrats are on the inside eating away at it. Then one day it all comes crumbling down.   Because the worthless local media did such a good job of covering it up, voters jaws are dropped in bemused wonderment, asking what happened, or how did this happen and no one warned us? The watch dog media turns out to be the watch out dog media. On the off chance Democrats do get the blame, they promise they will change, they never do; they never will.

Almost any day of the week, the media can report on some graft and corruption going on at city hall amongst Democrats, but they choose to look the other way. Yet, they make total hay out of every breath a Republican takes. They become the every breath you take police, and one infinitesimal nothing of a misstep by a Republican, becomes not only the local news lead story, but the national marxist media as well. While it takes them months (only after badgering by Rush Limbaugh, and Fox news) to do a courtesy glance at a Democrat scandal, they immediately make it the top story on their evening news broadcast. To these marxist malcontents being a Republican or Christian is criminal within itself. They want both outlawed the same way they do in communist countries.

During Bill Clintons two terms, the media routinely covered up his "scandal gates" a minute presidency. Back then it was more important to "feed a hungry child" than to get to the bottom of any of his many transgressions. We fast forward to today and find the same blind eye treatment of Barak Obama's, regime. Most Americans either have not heard of, or know very little about Benghazi, IRS targeting conservative groups, Fast and Furious, nor Solyndra. They are more interested in his basketball picks. Most of what the American people do know, they've learned from talk radio, Fox news, and the internet. What little the marxist media reports is given, not with a teaspoon of salt, but a jar of sugar.

A hee-hee and a ha-ha and: a keep moving folks there's
nothing here to see.   Nothing major or criminal happened
here, is how their reports are given. There is no furrowed brow
and deep serious monotone voice.   They may even flash a
personality.   As far at their text goes they might as well be
reporting on Justin Bieber, not some god awful president and
his equally bad Attorney General, yet again, wiping their half
Black asses with the Constitution of the United States.   But
let some burglars break into some unstable guy's psychiatrist
office, and they run a Republican president out of office.   We
are still hearing about Watergate, seemingly, a hundred years
later as if it just happened.   Every year we get the Woodward
and Bernstein, annual anthem and re-cap.   Men with the
personalities of a desk drawer tell us nothing new, year after
year.   What part Republican president Richard Nixon, may or
may not have had in the Watergate break-ins, in his six years
in office, doesn't begin to proach what Democrat presidents
(dictators) Clinton and Obama did in their first months in
office, much more thereafter.

Nixon's, six degrees of separation from the Watergate
burglars didn't stop the marxist news media or "feeble snobs"
then from calling it a "miscarriage of justice" a "detriment to
the country and Constitution," a "major cover up and scandal"
and an "abuse of power".   Yet, Obama's and Clinton's abuse
of power, and impeachable offense a minute are met with a
collective yawn by the marxist media.   They fidget more
over what's for lunch than covering Democrats, with any kind
of curiosity or jaundice eye. Because in their world view, it's
no biggie.   Just like being a Republican or Christian alone is
a criminal offense, no matter what it is a Democrat decides to
do illegal or otherwise, it automatically becomes okay.

Because in the tradition of Karl Marx, who cared for the poor people, it's perfectly okay because Democrats care. They and only they set the standard for what is right and wrong and they allow themselves space to decide on a case by case basis. Situational ethics is their birthright. They are god, thus arbiters of morality. When a Republican, points out a criminal offense by a Democrat and says it might be something wrong or untoward about it, the marxist media cancels lunch plans to attack him or her for pointing it out. Calling him or her a "partisan" on a "witch hunt" by crying "character assassination" and "distracting the voters". They do no investigation, not even a look-see to determine criminality. They just read the regime's prepared copy on the air and announce to voters nothing happened, so leave it alone.

In the same tradition of local Democrats and big city party bosses, robbing of the public trust and trough Obama, has taken Democrat party theft of public property to a height not even a Chicago precinct boss or a New Jersey mayor, could imagine. On behalf of Democrat party fat cats and donors with schemes so fraudulent that they would make the business practices of Tiggs/Ponzi/and Madoff P.O.P. (Pyramids-O-Plenty) investment firm seem sound, the Obama regime has done just that. Solyndra alone, almost a billion dollars was funneled into an investment scheme that no bank president in the world would float a short term loan of ten dollars without the full faith and credit of the United States behind it, at least what's left of its credit rating. Initially, the regime and the marxist media tried to blame George Bush. Many other of these payoff or kick-back schemes have been made to Democrat donors, even foreign nationals. They all went belly up inside of a year, with no sign of the billions of taxpayer dollars Obama loaned or invested in sight.

Obama's QE2 Federal Reserve scheme, feeds Wall Street or the New York stock exchange billions upon billions of useless printed notes, in order to create the illusion that the economy is doing good at the same time loading his investor class buddies like Warren Buffet, and other fat cat campaign donors with billions of American negotiable bank notes. Obama's "quantitative easing" scam is akin to feeding a three month old baby a pound of sugar a day with no solid food or formula to speak of.   While the newborn may enjoy it at first, even the most ardent of pro-baby killers can tell you this is not good for the baby, and if continued, will make the baby very sick or kill it.   There is no underlying economic or business activity to support any rise in the stock market, much less record breaking ones.   What we have is a whole lot of useless sweet paper, thus, the economic bubble.   A pro-baby killer and marxist like Barak Obama, wouldn't care if the baby died or the New York stock exchange, the cradle of capitalism, crashed and died either.

Most of us recognize that the marxist media are dumb as dirt people who are too lazy to learn or understand the intricacies of Fast and Furious, Solydra and QE2...

Note: The word of God says "if you hate your brother you are a murderer". Cain hated his brother Abel so he killed him.   Much the same way white liberals hate Black people and would love to see them exterminated.   Here are some other things liberals and the marxist news media hate: Jesus Christ, the cross, Christians, Catholics, Christmas, conservatives, conservation, colored people, the

Constitution, community, capitalism, cops, commerce,
concern for others, children, country, country-men,
economic classes, citizenship and chivalry. All these they
try and kill at every turn. Here are the things they love:
communism, communist, cancer, (breast cancer is caused by
abortions), corruption, careless Democrat presidents,
caustic behavior, callousness, contraception (especially
when abortions is the method) communals, crap, crisis,
economic collapse, crabby people, kooky causes and same
sex couples. All these they promote at every turn.

...It's easier for them to use the press clippings or copy given them by the Obama regime, to read to their dwindling audiences about the latest scandal or Keynesian attack on our economy. After all, nobody got hurt. No harm, no foul. The Constitution may be a little more tattered, who cares? According to marxist liberals, it's an old worn out piece of paper anyway. Besides, Obama wants to replace it with his declaration of "negative rights or liberties," which is slang for Bill of "no" Rights. Again, the media is too damn dirt dumb to understand that this will give a tyrant like Barak "insane" Obama, the right to confiscate people's personal property under the ruse of redistributing it to those he deems more worthy. What dumb-ass media types can't figure out is this puts us on a slippery slope in which a tyrant called Barak Hussein Obama rids them of their rights as reporters. It's easy as heck for us country bumpkins to figure out where all this ends up. But, people with diplomas, degrees and doctorates from Ivy League schools, having a combine IQ of two, can't. Shakespeare said: "first let's kill the lawyers." Once in total power tyrants say: first let's kill the reporters.

The Constitution they have all of this disdain for is what keeps them free to do their half ass job of reporting.   They should be the first to scream the loudest when somebody infringes upon it.   For some reason they can't get their heads out of their asses to see that.   Instead, the utterly worthless marxist media celebrate every diluting of it by tyrants like Barak Hussein Obama.

Welcome to the Machine:

There is no cover they won't throw over, or no flashlight they won't turn off in order to hide the glaring incompetents of Barak Obama.   They protect the maniacal three year old with everything they have.   But alas, here comes Obamacare, no longer does no harm no foul work; no longer does nobody got hurt work; no longer does nobody knows how bad they got hurt work; no longer does nobody cares work.   No longer does no one was affected work; no longer does the people are too stupid to understand what happened work; no longer does let's just pretend it didn't happen work.   No longer does spin work.   No longer can they change the subject work.   No longer can they count on the short attention span of the American people, and worst of all they can't even blame the Republicans.   Though they will try.   They might get ten years in a row Democrat of the year, Republican senator John McCain, to apologize on behalf of Republicans for passing Obamacare and bungling its implementation.   They might incentivize it and offer him a tour of the New York Times, parking lot.   After all, it's his mecca.   For this opportunity of a lifetime McCain will gladly drop trow, bend over, and let them sodomize him with this giant lie.

The rooster has come home to hatch this rotten egg laid by Obama the Democrats, and the marxist news media. Unless we have forgotten, no Republican voted to pass Obamacare, only Democrats. Even McCain didn't get near voting for this monstrosity. This is Obama, the Democrats and the marxist news media's baby. Both, the marxist media and the Democrats followed Obama's lead. Obama would say: "if you like your doctor, you can keep your doctor." The Democrats and the marxist media would repeat it verbatim. It was the same thing when Obama said: "if you like your insurance plan, you can keep your insurance plan." Obama would say: "Medical cost will go down tremendously," Once more, the mocking birds would sing along in perfect harmony. They all function as ventriloquist dolls with Obama's hand up their asses. Turns out, it was all a lie. Just like the Limbaughs, Hannitys, and Becks of the world, repeatedly said they were. While we couldn't expect dumb ass media types to know Obama was lying, us with a modicum of common sense knew from the start. Why pass a 2500 page legaleed law if nothing was going to change. Anybody who has had trouble balancing a check book could figure out that the numbers given didn't add up. The number of new insuree's, the number of doctors, the cost estimates, the number of participating doctors and hospitals. Anyone with a pencil and paper could have easily done the math on this. But, the thing that screamed the loudest, was it wasn't anything wrong with our health care system in the first place. Certainly, nothing that would take 2500 pages of small print to fix. What it needed was tort reform. But this awful bill let the ambulance chasers continue to run wild. I do believe it's very unfair and insensitive to expect the mentally challenged children in the marxist media to figure this out.

Still, they are faced with the monumental task of convincing Americans to ignore the man behind the curtain. In the next months we will think we are in la-la land or bazzaro world listening to the marxist media tell us to ignore the giant elephant in the china shop.   All the broke dishes and lives will be just a figment of our imagination.   All the broken promises were never promised in the first place. Republicans passed Obamacare, Democrat's tried to stop them.   Obama wants to repeal Obamacare but the Republicans want let him. Your insurance cancellations are actually Publisher's Clearing House prize notifications.   So go claim your prizes.   If they don't pay up Attorney General Eric Holder, will launch an investigation and see why they won't pay up.   You better believe some form of history revisionism or rewrite will take place.   More lies are all they've got.   Lies are all they ever had.

There is no kicking sand over this giant turd.   Even if you could, the smell is too massive to hide.   This is what we get for voting Democrat.   It would be fun to watch these lying Olympics, both by the marxist media and Obama, if it wasn't for the millions of Americans that no longer have health insurance and access to healthcare providers.   This smelly turd landed right in their laps.   No amount of brainwashing is going to tell them it's not there.   So they will need to shift the blame as to who defecated it.   Their usual spingalli: "That's rain not Democrats pissing on you" abracadabra pixie dust won't have the usual charm nor appeal it usually has for the sucker-moms.   Even the rudderless independents will have trouble being enchanted by this con offensive.   The string of yarn that can keep a kitten busy or distracted all day may not satisfy this time. Even American Idol, and the Kardashian's can't run on every TV channel all day everyday up until the next election, to keep the idiots distracted. I find it hard to believe that even the class envy, most dooped Democrat voter, can be shined on with tasty treats of schaden-freude of better off Americans not having healthcare. Then again, with these doops, the piss on them has always felt like rain.

    The American people want buy this is not happening to them. This is not the usual abstract manucial that goes on in that far away country called Washington D.C. Where we watch the machine out of the corner of our eye. Where the cobs turn, the levels go up and down, and the pendulum swings back and forth. That nobody pays much attention to, because nobody cares. But, this is real rubber hit's the road stuff. No insurance, no doctors, no healthcare. This ain't banning light bulbs, legislating the size of toilet tanks, raising the tax on cigarettes, or naming parks and battleships. This ain't happening in a far off land; this sausage making inner workings is right in the face and nostrils of Americans. This is unnerving. There is no comfortably numb state of being, here. Only more bricks falling off the wall and shoes to drop. It may be too late to have a cigar. There will be no turning away because we might run out of money. Still, the fleeting glimpse is right before our eyes. There may not be no doctor's pinprick to stop our fever and to hold us for a shout. So if you never cared a wit about Washington D. C., you do now. WELCOME TO THE MACHINE.

Note: Thomas Jefferson wrote… "Cherish therefore the spirit of our people, and keep alive their attention. Do not be severe upon their errors, but reclaim them by enlightening them.   If once they become inattentive to the public affairs, you and I, and congress and assemblies, Judge and governors shall all become wolves.   It seems to be the law of our general nature."

If the revisionist history attack doesn't work, at some point the marxist media will have to turn on Barak Obama, in order to save the party and whatever credibility they think they might still have.   The party is more important than some passing fancy.   They will nuance an attack against his Black half, not his marxist policies.   They might pull Jesse Jackson, out of moth balls to cut off his nuts. The Black one. One thing for sure the underside of a Greyhound bus is in his future.   More than this, the racist marxist media can't allow the smell of a "successful" Black man to linger in the air for too long.

Marxism

For those who have closely followed politics for the last sixty or so years with a jaundice eye on Democrats, and a realistic eye on history can easily know or predict the so called progressive's end game.   In short, the Democrats want to enslave us all.   Nothing short of complete control over our lives will suffice.   They have with the murder of more than 50 million people in their mother's womb, mentally and emotionally prepared themselves to kill, murder, imprison, and assassinate as many Americans as needed, to gain the absolute power they crave.   The maniacal power Russian madmen Joseph Stalin, Adolf Hitler, and Mao Zedong, had is their heart's content.   The only thing that separates these murdering butchers from those in America today is the time of century they lived in. Historical butcher's dictatorial murderous nature lives on in todays Democrat party.

Over the last years they have incrementally ran dry ruins on how much of our freedom they can encroach upon without us noticing or raising holy hell.   A case study is cigarette smoking.   How at the start they put an innocent enough "cancer is hazardous to your health" warning label on the side of the pack.   This started back in the mid sixty's.   Fast forward until today, now you can't smoke when and where you want to.   Some municipalities don't' allow you to smoke in your own home, nor at parks and on public benches out in the open air.   Restaurant owners are not allowed to have smoking sections in their own establishments.   One pack of cigarettes now cost more than $6.00 a pack.   Fat cat Democrat party trial lawyers have made hundreds of millions of dollars suing big tobacco on behalf of people who smoked themselves sick, even after seeing the warning on the side of the pack for over thirty years.   Those trial lawyers with help from the Democrat party and the marxist media managed to convince dumb ass jury members it wasn't' their clients fault their health was failing, it was big tobacco's fault. Even after seeing the warning label every time they went to light up.

There are those idiots or busy bodies that think all the rights lost over cigarette smoking is a good thing.   As someone who believes cigarette smoking is one of the dumbest things a person can do, I also believe it's none of my damn business if someone else smokes.   When someone lights up around me, I part their company.   I don't ask them to leave mine.   I allow them their freedom to smoke, at the same time maintaining my right to walk away.   It's win win.   In what's left of a free society the busy bodies must understand, there's something more sinister at work here, and has been for a long time.   All of this cigarette talk, banning this, banning that, is nothing more than dry runs on how much more of our freedoms they can secretly or openly get us to fork over under the guise of healthcare savings or second hand smoke is somehow killing someone else. This lie was solidified under Bill Clinton's administration. Then the marxist media ran with the lie. The useful idiot's fell for the lie. Even after the lie was proving to be a lie, the lie still managed to put hundreds of millions of dollars into Democrat trial lawyer pockets, thus into Democrat Party campaign coffers. Knowing logic is a hard concept to understand with liberals. If it takes a person 20-30 years of smoking to realize health issues, then how does someone healthy not smoking suddenly drop dead from inhaling second hand smoke. Is second hand smoke laced with potassium cyanide? The lie said that more than 3,000 second hand smoke fatalities took place a year. We would never expect the dumb asses in the media to ever figure out this was a gigantic lie, they just believe what they are told to believe by their Democrat party handlers. Joe Six Pack, should have picked it up off the bat. Now that we have a pack a day Democrat president suddenly the rage against smoking has ceased. It's no longer the scurge of western civilization. This is how it works with Democrats and the marxist media. They will never apologize for being hypocrites. To paraphrase Pastor Martin, I didn't do a doggone thing when they went after someone else, now they're hot on my trail and no ones left to help me. They attack cigarette smoking today, what the busy body likes to do, they might come after tomorrow. Then use that to separate us even further.

These marxist are patient with their march on freedom. Karl Marx, and Fredrich Engel living in Germany wrote the

"Communist Manifesto" in 1848.   It was some seventy years later when the Bolsheviks or left wing majority came to power in Russia under the tutorship of Vladimir Lenin, in 1917. The so-called October Revolution, made Russia the first proclaimed Communist State.   This came after seventy years of campaigning, organizing, protesting, publishing, speeches, agitating and propagandizing all over Eastern Europe.

Even though Karl Marx, wasn't a utopian (calling it "an abstract exaggerated sense of human possibility") he was a "radical theorist".   His theories of "higher-phase" communism and "lower-phase" communism (lower phrase being socialism, higher phrase being full blown communism), said once the productive forces were developed and capitalism was over thrown, would lead to an "abundant access to final goods."   Marx's theories of a quasi-utopian state has had a hundred years to play-out or manifesto in places like China, the USSR, Cuba, and Vietnam.   His theories are directly responsible for the deaths of near one hundred million people by murder, starvation, torture, disease and imprisonment.

In all of Karl Marx's fanciful writings and theories on a collective state, he totally ignored human nature.   Humans first of all yearn to be free.   Secondly, humans don't care for sameness, by nature they are individuals.   Thirdly, humans are always after a higher plane.   Fourthly, humans want the luxury of what they work for.   While charitable, they desire more than anything to enjoy the rewards of their own labor and not from someone else's "ability".   Definitely, they don't' want to put it in some communal pot for redistribution. Look at the extent humans have gone through to escape communist regimes.   That's why great walls, fences and iron curtains are erected to keep them in. There are no such enclosures around capitalist countries especially America. Still, no one tries to escape, not even the marxist. Wish they would. Marx, never considered those in charge of the pot would want all that's in the pot for themselves and would murder millions of people and their children to get and keep it. Others would simply sit down on their asses and wait for someone else to work and fill it. The collectivism theory nearly wiped-out the early American settlers by starvation. The pilgrims tried it, when it came time to putting it in the pot, nobody had tilled the soil or planted anything; each waiting for the other to work and fill it. That was when capitalism was born in American in the 1620's, and the first Thanksgiving came thereafter.

All Marx's theories of advantaging the proleriat by destroying the ruling class and capitalism has only led to the workers dying or becoming worse off. Whereas the ruling class capitalist land on their feet and becoming richer by escaping to other countries. His theories are only alive in the heads of college professors and so-called intellectuals. I mean how smart are you if you still believe communism is a viable solution to world problems. Communism alone with radical Islam, are the world's problems. Still, its beat-off to in college class rooms and faculty lounges, at disinformation universities of "lower phase" learning all around the country. Even though it is "an abstract historical exaggeration of human possibility."

Karl Marx's legaleze's, poetic flow, and intellectual flaunt leaves admirers saying "I don't know what he's talking about, but, it sounds good, let's try it." The only time Marx's theory of a communal enterprise has ever worked is at a large outside concert gathering like Woodstock.   It had plenty of communal sharing of body fluids, food and plenty of redistributionary pot.   After several days it was over and the participants were all worse for wear, headed back to the real world.   Strangely, the only time redistribution works is in the family dynamic. The working class proleriat husband goes out to work each day; the wife stays home and takes care of the children or "self actualize".   Then the father's "ability" allows him to redistribute to the family's "need" in the form of shelter, food and clothing.   Then he distributes to the wants: money, cars, jewelry, play stations…, etc.   Marx had a wife and six kids.   Why didn't he get this?   So if Marx himself didn't understand marxism, how then can we expect his modern day disciples and admirers to?

Karl Marx, never got to see his giant communal experiment materialize into full blow.   He never saw mass murderers like Joseph Stalin, Mao Zedong, Adolf Hitler, Pol-pot and Fidel Castro (and, if we don't pray, humble ourselves and turn from our wicked ways: Barak Obama) put his theories to work.   But, what his now disciples and admirers have is 20/20 hindsight.   No amount of "legaleed, poetic flow and intellectual flaunts" can cover-up the monumental disastrous failure communism has been to hundreds of millions of people throughout the world.   For almost a hundred years now, we have seen the Godzilla in Tokyo rampage disaster it has reeked on humanity.   Marx, never got to see his seventh baby grow up, we have.   Still, college professors, politicians and "Enlighten" intellectuals believe communism is a laudible goal and solution.

In this country we have had communism's younger brother "do good liberalism." Ever since Democrat president

Franklin D. Roosevelt's "New Deal" (1930's), and later on Democrat president Lyndon Bain Johnson's, "Great Society" (1965). Both have had disastrous effects on people in this country especially those in the Black family and community. Even after wealth transfers of $15 trillion…

Note: These roads to destruction have not been paved with good intentions, but, purposeful malice in order to take out an entire race of people.   White liberals and their house-niggers (Civil Rights cabal) started by removing the patriarchal structure of the Black community then they made sure Black women had cheap or free easy access to abortions.   Though, Black women are less than 8% of the population of the United States, almost 90% of plan parenthood, murder or abortion mills are located in and around Black communities. This is no accident, it is purposeful.   More than 1 out of 4 abortions are Black babies.   In some states it's as high as 2 out of 4, depriving the Black community of 25% - 35% of its population.   This program was originally designed by Margarett Sanger, for less desirables of an "unfit, irresponsible and reckless nature."   Blacks "whose religious scruples" prevent them from exercising control over their numbers"….., there is no doubt in the minds of all thinking people that the procreation of this group should be stopped."   Margarett Sanger, was the founder of Plan Parenthood.   Who gives more than 95% of its campaign contributions to Democrats?   Even though it was Richard Nixon, in an effort to make nice with Democrats that signed the so-called "Title X" legislation in 1970 that gave abortion subsidiaries

to poor women. Most assuredly, the "X" stands for "ex"
termination of Black people.   It's a pun that's not funny,
but tragic.

...With $15 trillion in transfer payments, they've only
propagated the problems they pretend to solve.   Still, the total
body of liberal thought is: let's do some more.

   With a long history of what should be eye opening
evidence, liberalism doesn't work, at any station or tenant in
the positive, leaves me to believe they want the disaster of
their programs or pogroms.   You will get no argument from
me that liberals are the dumbest and darkest brood of
"enlightens" amongst us.   Still, we have to wonder if they are
this dumb.   Maybe the rank and file members of the liberal
movement hadn't realized its cause as a giant failure, but the
leaders sell us this cock and bull lie day in and day out.   I
would never call Karl Marx, a snake-oil salesman.   He really
believed that his communist elixir was the right opiate for the
masses.   He really believed that the abolition of capitalism
would produce the economic engine needed to clothe and feed
the proleriat.   He dedicated his life to its design.   Even with
only foresight to glean from, his theories were a 180 degrees
out of phase with common sense and reality.   Marx didn't
have the hindsight of cause and affect but, his latter day
disciples do.   There are too many books, films, witnesses,
records, evidence, dead bodies and recent history to illustrate
that communism or any version thereof produces nothing
more than misery for the masses.   So why do big government
types still promote it as a viable solution to man's woes?   It's

simple, it puts them in charge of the "means of production," the workers, the factories, the raw materials, the military, and the imaginary redistributionary pot or lock box as comrade Hillary, would call it.   Then the individuals no longer are in control of nothing, even their own lives.   Everything and everybody belongs to a central government.   That's why the likes of Barak Obama, and his party hate capitalism.   It sets the individual free to peak his or her God given talents and gifts. Maximizing ones potential is a yearn of the human spirit.   Gaining as much wealth and security as possible within lawful parameters as a prize of endeavor called risk, reward, and hard work, without interference or injury from government is capitalisms nutshell.   Scottish born moral philosopher and economist Adam Smith, (1723-1790) believed that individual freedom was rooted in self-reliance and the ability to pursue his self-interest while commanding himself according to natural law.

Even though liberals and leftist hate the free exchange of labor, goods and money amongst a free people no one is hurt. There is a communal benefit to self-interest.   The baker rises early in the morning to bake bread or pies for his customers, mainly for profit.   There are three reasons people buy bread from the baker; either they don't have time to bake fresh bread in the mornings, or they don't know how to bake bread, and they like or need bread.   One or all three brings them to the bakers shop.   Now the customer can buy the bread, eat the bread, or he can call the baker an imperialist capitalist bastard and walk away hungry. Only a demented marxist or a "occupy wall streeter" do the latter.   The bakers reward is twofold, he gets the profit or money and the satisfaction or bonus of seeing others enjoy his bread or other confectioners treats.

Smith, said that was a principle in man…"that interest him in the fortunes of others, and render their happiness necessary to him, though he derives nothing from it, except the pleasure of seeing it."

The sentiment of seeing others happy is out of liberals and leftist ability to know.   They have no sense of honor nor natural affection.   They're hate and disdain for man collapses their ability to reference the principle.   This is why they spend inordinate amounts of time saying how much they care for the downtrodden or the poor and misfortunate.   Somehow they think we know it's all from the lips and not the heart.

Note: Democrats recognized long ago, Black folk suffered post slavery Stockholm syndrome. So we were starved for love and attention.   They knew from the beginning, that all was needed, was to say "I care." There's no shortage of racial self-pity. At the end of kicking us around like an old beer can, all we needed to hear was "I care." Then they could continue treating us like wolded gum stuck to the bottom of their shoes, and that we would remain loyal.

You can ask them the score of last night's game and with robotic rant, they launch into lip service of how much they want to help the poor.   My God man!   Take a minute off. When they're not talking about all the love they have for humanity they are running down Republicans and capitalism and thus, the people they serve which is everybody alive.   To a marxist liberal both are enemies of the state unless you are a

Warren Buffet, Steven Spielberg, or Jeffrey Katzenberger. There's not a speech that goes by that Barack Obama, doesn't take a cheap shot at capitalism. Since he's clueless, cheap shots are easy.

One can only marvel at the disconnect liberals and marxist have with capitalism and its patrons which is every living person on the face of the earth. On the one hand they "love" people, but on the other, they hate the very economic theory that causes them comfort and survivor; at the same time holding dear the one called communism which has only caused utter misery and death to mankind. No one can sit in a room in their house whether the den, kitchen, bathroom, home office, or a bedroom. We can't look in our refrigerators, nor cupboards or medicine cabinets, furniture, pictures, jobs, doors, windows and see nothing that wasn't brought to us without the engine of capitalism and its freedom. Our homes themselves, the wood, the bricks, the mortar, the nails, the sheet rock, the paneling, the flooring, the carpet, the linoleum, the paint, the shingles, the carpenters, our clothes, shoes, watches, computer, IPads, phones, cars, gas, oil, stop signs, caution lights, paved highways, paved streets. The only thing capitalism didn't bring us is the air we breathe, the oceans we visit, the clouds and other stellar beings we admire. Obama is not responsible for none of it. He just demoguse the hell out of it all. Even Obama's stash and even Obama phones, came through a free enterprise flow. The only thing communism produces is guns and bullets. They keep these aimed at the people.

NOTE: The government's function in it all is to make sure

everyone has the right to proceed with their risk or endeavor. The government is that New York City traffic policeman that stands in the middle of a busy intersection and directs the traffic.   His objective is not to stop traffic, but, to make sure it flows in a safe efficient way and that everybody gets to where it is they are trying to go quick, yet safe.   Communist on the other hand erects a wall or fence at that intersection and unless you have the "proper papers" which may take you months or years to get, depending upon what party official you manage to bribe to get them, you can't proceed.   Then those "proper papers" only get you to the next road block where a hold new set of "proper papers" are needed before you proceed.   By now the perishable goods you were trying to get to the market are now ruin. You have no profit and the customer has no decent food. The ones who get to bribe the local party official get his bread and butter to the market on time.   Since there's no competition there from other suppliers, he gets to sell his for exorbitant prices. Anyone who's ever tried to import fruit and other produce into California, knows what I am talking about. Now the customer gets to buy only half a loaf for the same price of five loaves. Walmart or any other grocer would gladly sale you a $20.00 loaf of bread, but other suppliers because they are allowed to exist without interference from the government would undercut their prices and Walmart's bread will sit on the shelves and eventually rot, because no one would buy it.   This is simply the law of supply and demand.   The greater the supply the lesser the cost of a product.   The greater the demand, the higher the cost may be, unless other suppliers are not allowed to come on line and dry up the additional demand.

Or existing ones are not allowed to ramp up manufacturing to meet the increasing demand. Someone paid $525,000 for a 1918, 24 cent Jenny stamp in 2005. Someone else paid $240 million for a 1888 painting of two men playing cards by French artist Paul Cezanne in 2011. Neither of the items carry value outside of its rarity, and how some rich guy with too much money and time on their hands bids up the price. A good professional ball player may make on average $2.5 million dollars a year. A teacher may average $55,000. In free market parlance or short thrift, teachers are a dime a dozen. If one teacher want take the $55,000 human resources has a thousand other applications. Some of those may even take less. Those that want, are free to venture into other avenues of making a living. These eventually become entrepreneurs. On the other hand only a hand full of people in the world can consistently break seventy on a golf course. Impressed with this fete, tens of thousands of patrons or fans might pay between $25 and several thousand dollars to watch golf up close and personal, not to mention the millions who might watch on television. Whenever a Mickelson or Woods, is in the field these numbers might double. Between ticket sales and advertising revenue, the event planner and the television network might clean up $20 or more million dollars just for that Sunday, not to mention the other three broadcast days. From the last place to the first place golfer, between $25,000 and $850,000 dollars is made. The money the last place golfer will make is almost half that for four days work, what a teacher will make in a year. It's the same with a winning quarterback or, 1,000 yard rusher in football, or a high scoring basketball player; and a 90 mile an hour *pitcher or a .300 average batter in baseball. Their talents are so unique or their supply is so rare fans or the demand, are willing to pay a lot of money for tickets to see them, or are grip to their television sets to watch them. The more eyes on a particular event the more networks can charge sponsors for a 30 second commercial. So it is with actors and other entertainers. It seems so unfair especially in light of the fact that all of these athletes and entertainers had to come through a teacher to get to where they are. One thing is for sure no one is going to pay to watch me play golf. Maybe to go away. Neither would they pay to see me acting in a movie or play. Again, maybe to go away. No one is going to pay to watch a teacher teach. Most of the audience they already have don't want to be there. Yet, all of us owe our success in part or whole to teachers. Throwing, catching, or hitting some spherical object doesn't begin to approximate their contribution to our society. Where we mess up is when we ask or allow politicians to make it all "fair" or "equal" or make them come see me play golf. Then we will end up with no teachers, no athletes, and when you give them permission to start meddling in the free market you will have no bread and no butter. Milton Friedman said: "If you put the government in charge of the Sahara Desert, in 5 years you will have a shortage of sand."*

…My guess is, when the doors are shut, the blinds are roll shut, the curtains are drawn; the mix company is gone, liberals let their hair down and scream to the top of their lungs

"NIGGER!", "NIGGER!", "NIGGER!" to release the tension of playing nice to Black folk for long periods of time without decompressing. In much the same way Bill, Hillary, and Roger Clinton did in Arkansas, and Washington D.C. We know that they threw around the "N" word like they did favors for their crony friends. A return to slavery is always at Democrats, hearts door. So they have to repeatedly rehearse that they care so much for Black people they fear a public slip of the tongue; or I could say slip of the heart. What's in the heart of Democrats is hate and racism. Out of the abundance of the heart, they try hard not to say it.

They see capitalism in the same light they view Christianity. Both are impediments to their final solution of enslaving us all. Free people engaging in the free exchange of goods services and money; believing in a higher power other than Democrats, is Dracula meets cross for them. They recoil at their existence. Karl Marx being a descendent of the rabbinical priest line, but raised Lutheran didn't hate religion. He believed though delusional or "illusory" was still a necessary escape from "distress or protest against real suffering" for the poor. I believe, if alive Marx would be horrified at the devastation his theories have reaked on mankind. He would repent of his inane theories the same way Charles Darwin, did his. Equally terrifying to him would be how modern day so-called intellectuals pant for the implementation of his insane theories. Even with the benefit of 20/20 hindsight, these anti-lectuals are either dumb as hell or evil as hell, neither is acceptable. Much learning has made these people mad. Unlike Marx, todays liberal and marxist vile the very thought of the Judeo-Christian ethic. Sin is a stench in the nostrils of God and God is a stench in the nostril of today's marxist.   Anything that puts them out of the realm of God or vanishes their exaltation of their throne above that of God's is simply an oppressive injustice brought on by the capitalist pigs.   They want us to choose them over God. God is that creator and life-giving and sustaining force.   That all of the universe and universes and their characters are powered by.   He can dangle the sun as if it were a yo-yo. Only He has the keys to life being abundant and to Heaven's gate.   What are the liberals offering that we should appease them?   Like Slept-rock, everything these imps walk by or touch wilts and dies.   The inner cities, the Black family, the Black person, unborn babies, common decency, the economy, healthcare, jobs and education are projects they've taken under their wings, none can be called a success.   There is no sane reason to vote for Democrats.   Still, these narcissistic elites tolerate no rebellion and welcome no debate.   They pant for the day, there is no choice, their way or die.   Again, Democrats, are dirty, low down rat fink bastards who want to enslave us all.

THE HUMAN SPECIES:

I do believe some aspects of Marx clinical, non-spiritual, theoretical, yet humane treatment of human nature was on point.   He wrote humans were composed of "tendencies," "drives," "essential powers," and instincts to act in order to satisfy "needs" for external objectives.   He went on to say humans are involved in "all-round activity "all-round development of individuals" "free development of individuals." "The means of cultivating gifts in all directions." Marx believed man's nature was a "force"

"external" upon him that "drives" him to fulfill these
"external needs" and that a good society allows these
expressions. Surprisingly, he thought the homo-sapiens of
higher origin than the overall animal kingdom do to
"consciousness" and "religion."   Today's marxist would call
this heresy or apostasy in the first order, and impeachment
proceedings would began immediately.   Even if it was Karl
Marx that said it. No self-respecting liberal or marxist would
or should ever think someone outside their congress was
higher or smarter than an animal.   They think we are nothing
but animals so they get to treat us as such.   That's why an
unborn baby is nothing more than a glob of tissue at best, a
fetus.   Once the unborn is dehumanized then they get to treat
it as such.   They strongly believe they are above it all and
entitled to their perceived stratum and all of its accompanying
perks.   So much for the prejudice and arrogance of the
bourgeois or rich capitalist.

Marx believe this "species being" "life activities"
distinguished him from animals.   Animals only produce their
immediate needs and are one with its existing environment.
Man produces beyond his immediate needs to survive and
within his "life activities" or changes his environment. Man's
activity are "conscious" while animals are instinctive.   Man
is the tool making creator or homo sapiens he believed.

But where Marx starts to rear off the beat and path is in
his economic theories.   To my knowledge he never explains
how do you fit these five fingered "species beings", into his
one fingered communal glove without the force of state.   If
humans are these species that yearn to transform their
environment and are composed of "tendencies" "drives"
"essential powers" and instincts to act in order to satisfy needs

for "external object."   Then how do you get them to put the rewards of these drives, powers, and tendencies into this communal pot.   If survivor is the first order of man's nature, which proposes its subtitles of "dog eat dog," me, myself, and I, "I got mine you get yours, mine, mine, mine, and the invitations to go and make love to oneself," and to attach ones lips to another's posterity are ever present.   Then it becomes clear that the volunteer mechanism needed might require re-tooling.   Now a not so natural selection takes place. Given that liberals believe man is inherently greedy and selfish then how do you jive the two – human nature and the community pot, short of forced coercion?   You erect a monument call the IRS with full power to coerce, threaten, or hold a yard sale outside people's front door.

Then we ask, how does all of Marx's "self-actualization" "free expression" and "all-around activities" manifest without capitalism.   It is capitalism that clears the avenue to "self-actualization."   For example, I need dance lessons, voice lessons or whatever "I" decide to do toward "my" actualization goals.   All cost money.   Even the car ride over. Yes, under a communist regime, dance lesson might be free, but, "you" don't get to decide that you want to be the next Mikhail Baryshnikov, the state does.   Just as it decides who becomes an aero-space engineer, and who becomes a janitor. In most cases the engineer may end up a janitor.   The "individual" outside of big time communist party connections doesn't get to decide what direction "their life" takes, the state does.   A Britney Spears or a Justin Timberlake, doesn't get to decide to work hard and become mega pop stars.   They would be blessed not to be shipped off along with 6 million others to Siberia where the temperature average -40 degrees below zero to work in some gulag coal mine, until they drop dead. The only passion pursued by people under a communist regime is freedom.   They go under any curtain, climb over any wall and swim any ocean to escape it.

According to Marx, for communism to work capitalism and private property has to be eliminating.   How does anything get grown, produced, or manufactured now that the "means of production" are removed?   Marx believed that the elimination of the means of production would magically bring this euphoric state about with cumbala its national anthem, and harmonic convergence its holiday.   Then out of all of this anti-capitalist activity was to flow an "abundance of goods" and services.   Marx compiles the idiocy of his plan when he said work or labour are "unfree," "unhuman" and an "unsocial activity." "He called capitalism a "person" that exerts torment on the laborer."   The question remains with all of this self-expression going on, who will be working to pay the bills. Apparently, Marx's vision skipped the 20th century and went straight to the 21st, where everyone would have a "home food dispenser", a robot maid name Rosie, a pet name Astro and no Spacely Sprockets, to contend with.   Actually, the stone age would be a step up from Marx's, communal design once fully implemented. Living in a stoned house and working in a gravel pit would be a luxury. Your pet Dino might have been your last meal.

In addressing life under communism Marx gets really hippie-noctic.   He wrote: "In the individual expression of my life I would have directly created your expression of your life and therefore in my individual activity I would have directly confirmed and realized my true nature, my human nature, my communal nature."   What in the heck does this mean?   Ted

Kennedy's October 1994 campaign speech made more sense. We thought this flower child far out man New Age nutty talk was a more resent event. Apparently, genus cannabis isn't a recent event either. It should be noted Marx wanted labor eliminated under communism. No doubt, communism is a lazy man's religion. No one with a hammer and nail in hand is spending time stalling the virtues of communism, only tenured professors, trust funders and tenth year art students on full scholarships rap about its lofty tenants.

While young Carlos Santana, was "self-actualizing", practicing his guitar licks at home, someone either one or both his parents, or/and his several siblings had to be out working, providing young Carlos, food, shelter and clothing. Being a classic rock lover, I am glad they did. I learned to play air-guitar, later air-drums, and piano listening to it. All of these necessities don't get provided without someone entering some work place established by capitalist and their capital. It is "commodity fetishism" that makes the world go round. Money burns the engines to "semblance" or needs being met.

Capitalism allowed to flourish without government interference (high taxes and unnecessary burdensome regulations) makes more opportunity for the proleriat or laborer to find good paying jobs. So then, it becomes a workers market where they sell the only asset they have; their labor to the highest bidder. The job market now swings dramatically in their favor. The capitalist who offers only $10 an hour may not get his manufacturing done or widgets made, if the other widget makers are offering $15 or more an hour. Also, amongst the higher paying widget makers, in addition to a higher rate of pay, they offer benefits like health insurance, vacations and retirement plans as incentives to get and keep good workers.   All this is done without government lifting a finger.   Its call supply and demand, supply side, the free market, and free enterprise which marxist hate.   It doesn't cost the government anything to just get out of the way.   Then with all of these proleriats having good paying jobs, the tax receipts go up.   Now the government has more money to buy votes or social programs without running dangerously high deficits.   Unhindered capitalism is win win for all involved.   Greedy politicians will still demand more no matter how much money comes into the treasury.

The union bosses know this and that it affects their trough minutes.   So they fight for government interference. Without a limited amount of jobs, they have no jobs. They need workers frighten of the same "scarcity" Marx and his comrades said that capitalism causes in order to chorale and keep workers in the unions.   The lesson is, Marxist love money too, they just hate the idea of working for it.   It's easier to get government's heavy hand to confiscate it from others and give it to them or they erect a court system that exacts it from companies through vices called class action or liability law suits;   usually, for large amounts of money for little or no pain and suffering.   Companies are force to add these punitive cost back into the cost of goods sold.   We all end up paying for frivolous law suits.

When marxist are in full blow they generally kill their charges to accumulate wealth by working them to death. Under communism a forty hour work week will seem like a week's vacation.   You just don't work your hands to the bone, you work your entire body to nothing but skin and bones.   Then you die from starvation and exertion.   Under Marx's communist model work was supposed to be eliminated because the seeds to the communal money tree would seed themselves, plant themselves, fertilize and grow themselves; and like mushrooms or manna, we go outside the next morning and like magic it all appears.   All we would ever need; we want even have to slay and eat.   This is the cock and bull fantasy world Democrats present to the voters at every turn.   The idiots eat up this cradle to an early grave fault free living lie.   Just roll out of bed at your convenience and it will be there waiting on you: money, food and shelter. Just vote Democrat and the gravy train keeps on rolling.   Us with brains and a cursory knowledge of history, especially where communism is concern know that "do good liberalism" is just the first stop on the communist express as it rolls downhill from its peak of capitalism passing socialism. Its final stop or destination… communism.   Then a job in a freezing cold deep dark dirty dank coal mine in outer Siberia will be found for you.   No job application needed, no OHSA regulations and no union or shop steward's representation. No 30 minute lunch break, days off, no complaint department, no talking back to your supervisor.   Slave labor will be just you and the guard with the gun pointed at you.   Now I dare you to bitch about your civil rights or sinful rights.

While Marx's observations were subjective, maybe emotional, today's Marxist in charge of the Democrat party, are objective and compassionless.   Unlike Marx, they know the outcome of communism they've seen the end-game in all of its inglorious machinations.   Still, they say gimme, gimme.   Not for them, but for the rest of us.   Marx conjured that fee simple or owning private property was the reason for the "antagonism" between the classes.   Even the feudal system of lord and vassal was unacceptable to Marx.   But, neither bourgeois nor the proleriat were to blame for class struggles, it was the unions that made the strife and fan the flames of revolution often with assistance from standing governments.   Most people adopt a "live and let live" posture.   I am alright, jack…. just need your hands off of my stash.   Thomas Jefferson wrote that it was European governments that divided the nations into two classes "wolves and sheep."   As long as labor is fighting capitol the real problem, the antagonist called union bosses and government allies go free.   Then unfettered supply and demand activity goes on untried.   Then we all continue to lose out because of an inordinate foolish phobia about rising tides, baked into our heads by the marxist media and their Democrat Party handlers.

Saul Alinsky and His Disciples:

   Both Barak Obama, and Hillary Clinton's, mentor real time and posthumously was Sal Alinsky (1909-1972).   He dedicated his book "Rules for Radicals" to Lucifer, calling him the "first radical" to rebell against the establishment.   In his 1971 treacherous treatice on how to destabilize governments, seemingly just for kicks, Alinsky wrote "A Marxist begins with his prime truth that all evils are caused by the exploitation of the proleriat by the capitalist from this recognition then all action or ends and gains are necessarily from it…,proceeds the revolution to end capitalism."   Alinsky, said the only question of "ends" is whether they are "achievable" and the only thing unethical about "means" is their "non-use."   This rationale gave license to Obama's friend Bill Ayers, and his communist proclaimed "Weather

Underground", to go on a series of bombings in the late 60's early 70's inside the United States.   One such bombing killed three members of Ayer's terrorist group and wounded others.

The former Chicago community organizer's disciples were instructed to penetrate all aspects and spheres of influence and subvert them which explains, the marxist media, teacher's unions, courts, Hollywood, liberal pulpit preachers, the Democrat party, Hillary Clinton, Bill Clinton, and Barack Obama.   He suggested they shed their communist or radical attire "cut" their hair and wear "suits.", they needed to blend in.   So these wolves in sheep's clothing would look no different from you and I. With the advent of young Barack Obama, who "cut" his hair and began to wear "suits," these subversives have put on a body snatch invasion of the third kind.   As I write, their Kraken like tentacles are posed to choke the life out of capitalism and our country.   They are everywhere you look, the thing is you don't see them because they look like you and I.   They don't look like the walking dead or zombies they really are.   They are whited sepulchers, cold, heartless, and dead; yet with a sparkling personality.

Obama's manifold destructive moves were not out of incompetents.   This boy ain't as dumb as we give him credit for.   He is deliberate with every move, and calculating.   He knows the exact result of every action or "means" he takes. After all, while a communist organizer in Chicago, he taught Alinsky's destabilizing tactics.   He is a skilled marxist. Though flimsy on how many states there are.   I'll bet you 36¢ I can find almost two Harvard grad students that might know the answer.   Somehow his hatred for America and Alinsky's tutelage made him the pathogen we are diseased by today. Just because he spends most of his time playing golf, doesn't mean bad things aren't happening.   He's so good at tearing apart America, he makes it look effortless.   Then again, we are just sitting back allowing it all because we are afraid of being called racist.   In my case "sell out" or Uncle Tom.   I proudly bare the banner of both names if it means saving the country I love.   It is no great sacrifice. Thousands of others have given life and limb to save her.   The truth is "White racist", "sell outs", and "Uncle Toms" are primarily in the Democrat party.   Just a small quick peek at history then and now bares it out.   The late South Carolina's senator Strom Thurmond, says he left the Democrat or Dixie-crat party once he got saved and filled with the Holy Ghost, and went to the Republican Party because he no longer wanted to be a racist.

Thesis and Theory:

Hillary Clinton's nightmare for America is no different from Barak Obama's.   Saul Alinsky, was so impressed with her Marxist credentials he offered her a job.   She wrote her ninety-two page Wellesley College thesis, "There is only the fight" an analysis of the Alinsky model, as some sort of tribute to him. While critical of his approaches or "means" his "ends" were synonymous with hers.   The destruction of capitalism thus America were desired goals of both.   My insight of Hillary on Alinsky is that she felt the moral decay or "dialect process" at that point in America's history in the late 1900's hadn't reached the necessary critical mass needed to make Alinsky's "means", "achievable."   The Supreme Courts ban on school prayer (1962-1963) hadn't had its desired negative effects on our society…just yet.

Now having ditched her long stringy hair, sandals and

stripped bell bottoms in exchange for any designer's pants "suit" that will send her an invitation to whatever homosexual soiree or gala; now without the wholesale wonder lust for the White House, dominating whatever conscience she might have, she would gladly openly agree with Alinskys "means" and "ends". She wrote Alinsky's "… power/conflict model is rendered inapplicable by existing social conflicts" because "The once chrononistic nature of small autocronmous conflicts."   In laymen's: America at this point is not readily prepared to accept communism because of strong moral beliefs and patriotism, and no amount of protest and agitation by a few unshaved smelly freaks was going to change that.

   We know what Hillary's college thesis was about. What about young Barack Obama?   His college thesis at Columbia remains as illusive and mysterious as the Lochness Monster. In light of all he has done since becoming president what could he have written twenty five years ago that could cause anyone to rethink any opinion held positive or otherwise about him. Short of admitting he shot Kennedy; I don't see the big deal. The New York Times and the supposed professor who gave him an "A" on the paper, but couldn't remember exactly what it was about; try and sell us this cock and bull story that it was on Soviet Nuclear disarmament; and negotiating with the Russians.   Now, how many Americans, still clutching their right minds with everything they've got, believe that?   I would have a much easier time believing some nut-case account of his alien abduction; than young Barry wanting his mecca, communist Russia (not his Saudi Arabian Mecca) disarmed.   As president he has offered and given them a two for one trade off of most of our nuclear weapon systems.   Now that's how a good negotiator does it;

give the crazy people sitting across the table, bent on world domination, more than they could imagine asking for. We see the same negotiating prowess with the Iranians. Again, give the real crazy people sitting across the table bent on world destruction, all the nuclear bombs they could ask for.

During the Cold War, and even now, some Russian generals and Soviet Party members openly push for a sucker-punch nuclear strike against America. Just as U.S. general Curtis Lemay recommended we do to them. Some calculate a one and done scenario, where we don't have the stomach or backbone to respond in kind. Lord knows we don't have the leader that would. He might threaten to go to the U.N. They kick the M.A.D algorithm out of the equation for this reason. My understanding of Obama's hate for America, then and now, tells me if he wrote about Russia and nuclear armament, as his senior thesis, he was egging on this nuclear strike by the Russians. No doubt, Obama made an "A" on this paper. A mad man's mind is a mad man's garden. Given what we already know about Obama, nothing else could be damning to him. Maybe, not even this.

While we speculate and theorize on Obama's college thesis content, still, nothing divorces us from the belief that he is an unavowed Marxist bent on the destruction of America as we know it. His wife admitted it in every speech until they shut her up, which is no small fete for a Black woman. This isn't young Marxist doodling theories in a college thesis paper no more. This is right now in your face real life, real time, real serious. Darning "haircuts" and nice "suits", these Alinskyites have seized control of most of our lives. Judging by their previous moves we know their future ones will be every bit as destructive. WHAT WILL WE DO? There was that infamous prophesy, to some, "I hope he fails." Unfortunately, Obama, and the Democrats have very much succeeded in setting this nation on a collision course with plate smashing financial disaster, leaving themselves in place to pick up the pieces and rearrange them in the way they want to. Which will be communism, complete with death camps, concentration camps, forced labor camps and firing squads. Again, what will we do?   What are we prepared to do?

MIND GAMES:

What the Alinskyites, have been doing to America for over forty years now is running a psych op's campaign.   With the release of "Rules for Radicals" Alinsky and his disciples in effect declared war on America, with capitalism as its ruse. You can't openly declare war on America; even some liberals may find that problematic.   So you declare war on capitalism making it the focus of attack and everything that's wrong in the universe.   You don't say replace capitalism with communism.   Instead, you say: peace, love, the Age of Aquarius and good vibrations. This is the attraction for idealistic young minds. You don't tell these wannabe Alinskyites in what will become reality once capitalism is gone.   There will be no more hanging out with friends at the mall, movies, IPods, I Phone nor myself and I. No, you become just another lifeless cog in the communist state machine.   The Alinskyites know once you get rid of capitalism you get rid of America as we know it.   I love America as we know it.   These dark dank people know when you take away the light the darkness appears.   These love the night because their deeds are evil.   They can't attack us physically, especially since the downfall of communist Russia.   So they move into a psychological war and wear away at our rational thinking and moral fiber.

Former KGB operative and defector Yuri Bezemenov, (1939-1993) lectured back in the 80's on how the Soviet Union would bring down America.   He said that the KGB would do it not with guns or espionage, but, with "ideological subversion" and so called "active measures". He said while only15% of Soviet activities of gun power and espionage were outside of the Russian borders, 85% went to "distractive aggressive activity" aim at destroying nations or geographical areas.   He said the party members wasn't interested in a battlefield approach but by subverting our education system, our media, military, unions, and religious institutions. Bezemenov, said that the Soviets wasn't that interested in learning our secrets, but, to demoralize us.   As Obama constantly does. He said the KGB set forth a 15-20 year plan to demoralize us because that's how long it would take to warp the minds of a generation.   At some point, he noted, that you would "change the perception of reality" then "no one is able to come to a sensible conclusion about defending themselves their families nor country."   One of the tenants of demoralization would be to attack religion by "ridiculing" it and to "destroy" it by replacing it with occultism or sects. This is the same as Alinsky's "dialectic process". The aim he said was to "wear away at excepted dogma." Notice the rash of Harry Potter books and movies. The Democrat party, the news media, and Hollywood attacks accepted dogma all day every day.   They have done everything possible to ridicule and destroy traditional valves at every outing.   With multiple soft whispers, overtime they have attempted to subconsciously get Americans to believe there is no God, or concept of right and wrong; and that homosexuality is not an abomination condemned by God…but, a perfectly normal acceptable lifestyle choice. Not that there's anything wrong with it.

Notes: Homosexuality as well as lesbianism is an abomination.   There's nothing gay or GLAAD about it. From my vanish point, it's living a misery that I wouldn't want for my worst enemy.   The guilt and the shame covered over with drug and alcohol addictions, and many multiple sex partners must be unbearable.   Some might even want AIDS and die as a means to escape the emotional pain and humiliation of it all.   But, there's a loving God who sent His Son Jesus, to die for the homosexual and his sins. While we were yet sinners Christ died for us.   Jesus knows all about the shame the guilt and the humiliation.   More than anything he wants to forgive them of their sin and walk with them with love, kindness, patience, and longsuffering right out of this abomination.   Yes, Jesus loves the homosexual right where he is: in the muck and mire of his condition and sin.   He understands it.   So we don't have a High Priest that cannot be touched with the feelings of our infirmities; but was in all points tempted as we are, yet without sin. All the homosexual has to do is receive Jesus Christ, as their Lord and Savior, and trust him to bring a joy to their hearts, take away the suicidal tendencies and change their lives.   John Stossel knows nothing.   Jesus is the one that loves them so much he died

for them.   The demon vote seekers who tell the homosexual
he's okay in his or her abomination hates them.
Remember, hate is a prerequisite to becoming a good
Democrat.

These cold war remnants or Alinskyites have us arguing among ourselves almost to the point where we can't come to a consensus on how to protect ourselves, families and country.   A divided nation cannot stand.   They continuously beat us over the head with "tolerance"; specifically tolerating homosexuality and their arrogant behavior. At the same time, they tell us to hate Christians and morality. Just like the Nazi's Der Stürmer newspaper (The Attacker) browbeat the German people into voicing an unfavorable opinion of Jews in the mid 1930's; so does the marxiest media, Hollywood, and the pussies at ESPN try and brownbeat us into voicing a favorable opinion of homosexuality today. Our perceptions of reality have been warped by the subversive demoralization of the Alinskyite enemy among us.

The Alinskyite media antagonize us with racism at every turn. Almost everything is tagged as racist or having racial overtones.   It's getting to the point when a White person is found breathing it will be construed as racism by the Alinskyite media and the race-hustlers.   Not that they care about racism. They are the biggest most racist imps known to man.   It's just part of their pysch ops or brainwashing "active measures."   Always remember, Democrats were the original and only slaveowners in our nation's history.

CRITICAL MASS:

Just like they do with the homosexual questions, little by little, the Alinksyites have soft pedaled the virtues of being on the public dole and the selfishness and greed of those who want to keep more of their hard earned money for their families and themselves.   They have long started a campaign to demonize those who agree with the Tea Party, implying they are selfish racist bastards.   Sadly the alinskyites have been joined by some establishment Republicans in attacking the Tea Party for its stands on government waist and tyranny. While quarterback Barack Obama, and the Democrats run the "Rules for Radicals" playbook to the n'th degree, scoring a touchdown with every possession and the Republican team, with the exception of a few players, are on the side lines hiding from voters, afraid to come to a consensus on how to save America.   Running out the clock with the other team ahead is becoming more and more of their loosing strategy. They refuse to fight fire with nothing more than sprinkles of fear.

We have now reached a critical mass where the economic nexus of people in the wagon are about to outnumber the ones pulling the wagon.   Unemployment has become virtuous and stylish.   Work has become foolish. Marx's dream scenario becomes more and more of a reality. The Alinsky or Obama plan is this, wear out the fools still pulling the wagon by frustrating them with higher and higher taxes or destroy all means of capital structure or take control. Then, cause those still pulling the wagon to jump into the wagon overload the wagon or social safety net with welfare, disability and social security checks, cause the wheels to fall off or the net to split open with government entitlements, deficit spending then government bankruptcy.   Now you have the communist perfect storm: poor hungry destitute people by the hordes of millions with nowhere to go. Nothing from nothing always end up leaving nothing.   Now anarchy and rioting breaks out.   America resembles some "Thunder Dome apocalytic reality.   The bourgeois and the capitalist have flown their private jets to safe harbors or ports of call.   While the proleriat is living on the streets.   The dumb asses in the media have been choraled imprisoned or shot.   The media are generally the first to be taken captive when communist take over.   Sometimes you wonder if it all maybe worth it to see that.   In all of this confusion, Obama, now becomes Premier Leader and the United States military becomes the Red or pink army.   Then the tanks roll.

Note: As Chancellor of Germany, Adolf Hitler, in 1933 took advantage of a fire that broke out in the Reichstag to deprive the German people of their civil liberties and habeas corpus rights. Even though no one knew how the fire started, Hitler claimed the communist (code for Jews), calling it a ...."ruthless confrontation of Communist Party of Germany" He called for Germany's president Paul Von Hindenburg, to call a special session of the bi-cameral houses of the Reichstag and the Reichstrat of the Weimar Republic. After only 52 days as Chancellor, Hitler convinced both legislative bodies, ironically with a lot of religious verbiage, to fork over all their power to him, by passing so-called "Enabling acts". This gave Hitler plenary powers. In short, Hitler was handed dictatorial rule over the Weimar Republic without firing a shot.

With that, Hitler plunged the world into war where the estimates of those killed are as high as 85million. At least half of these were in Europe. This is reminiscent of how Democrats of both the senate and House of Representative gave Barack Obama dictatorial rule over our healthcare system. He will use "plenary" power to black mail the American people into giving him dictatorial rule over America. Obama maybe ignorant of a lot of things, but achieving dictatorial rule ain't one of them. He awaits his Tonkin opportunity. He is well studied on this subject. That's why he starts fires every chance he gets. But, in the words of Billy Joel, "We didn't start the fire", but we damn well gonna put it out!

Once the media is rounded up shot or imprisoned, then they roll on the homosexuals.   These are never far from the communist top of list round ups. Like Jews, homosexuals have always suffered the hardest under socialism and communism.

Note: Throughout the last century and a half, Jews and homosexuals have always been in the cross-hairs of freedom hating regimes.   In the 1930's, it was the Nazis in the Weimar Republic of Germany, that made the office of homosexual rights activist Magnus Hirshfeld, Scientific Humanitarian Committee its first stop on the way to Hitler's final solution.   Hitler took aim at Jews and homosexuals. Hirshfeld, was at large when the round up started, and never return to Germany. Jews and homosexuals have always been at the forefront of making socialism and communism happen. Yet, it has been Jews and homosexuals that have suffered the most. KGB defector Yuri Bezenemov, said homosexuals are the "first" to lose freedom under communist regimes. According to the Distributed Republic blog, Vladymir Lenin, thought homosexuality was a disease that needed to be cured, and force them into psychiatric hospitals. In Mao Zedong's China, they were forced into heterosexual marriages, or imprisoned. Cuba's Fidel Castro, called them "maricones" (faggots) and denounced them as "sexual deviants." Karl Marx was excoriated by his friend and co-author Friedrich Engels, for considering supporting the homosexual agenda. Engels, call them "pederast" or child molesters, who were "extremely against nature." He refered to their movement as "turning theory into smut." While Joseph Stalin, was somewhat lenient with Jews, he criminalized homosexuality in Russia, making it punishable by five years of hard labor.

While communism regards no man, it does seem to be this incessant need for both Jews and homosexuals to tilt at its windmill even when they are the first to get cut down by its blades.

It is quite understandable that pre-Bolshevic Jews wanted to rid Russia of its Csarist system of government. Given the rolling pogroms under czars like Catherine the Great (1762-1796) Alexander III (1881-1884) and Nicholis II (1884-1877), any kind of change seemed welcomed. But you don't replace one system of an unelected Czarist monarchy, with another non-elected central planning communist committee. The problem ain't people who govern within a system of checks and balances. It's people who wheel absolute power, with nothing or no one to answer to but, their non-existent consciences.   We've all heard it "absolute power corrupts" now it's time we all believed it and move away from this cult of personality mode.   We don't need another leader.   This is what makes Barak Obama, so dangerous by "changing" America as we know it, he totally ignores constituted laws without any consequences.   He's not afraid of congress nor the voters. The Democrats and courts ola' and cheer his every transgression of the Constitution, "Tyrants all!"

THE PARADOX OF PARADIGM CONNUMDRUMS AND DICHOTOMIES:

It has always disturbed me or has been a constant head-scratcher why both dig the hell out of socialism and communism because of some "stupid" workers right ruse. Are they not reading the same history books I am reading? Have they not heard of the Nationalist Socialist Party (Nazis)? Nobel Peace Prize winner economist Milton Friedman, said that it is the Jewish intellectual that has sort to "undermine" capitalism throughout history.   These have graduated and taught at the most prestigious universities in the world.   In my limited knowledge of academia is that you have to be smart to find yourself in its midst.   What seems easy for us lessers to figure out, seems impossible for the intellectual elites to grasp.   So in our bemusement we ask: what attracts the moth to the flame? What is it that keep the battered wife going back to her betrothed? Is there a Stockholm brand here? Maybe there's a competition amongst smart people to see who can be the dumbest. With the exception of a few, Jews put their support behind an economic theory that throughout history has been nothing but a miserable failure. I read Einstein's theory of insanity and I got it. While I am still working on $E=MC^2$, I understand and recognize insanity right off the bat. I know that any government tasked with central planning as a desire, is crazy. History is filled with communism's failure so earth's soil is filled with the blood of those that couldn't travail its tyrannical rule.

An essay or homework assignment becomes necessary for the intellectual, Jewish or otherwise. Using only one paragraph, and in plain English free of legaleed poetic flow, and intellectual flaunt, write for us the great things that have happen under communism. Don't romanticize as Karl Marx, did on its wonders and opiate elixir for the masses as theoretical pretzeling, but, what good has happen since its inception in the last hundred years. Inform us of its success or utopian state. You can't hide behind lofty idealism, as we've heard that gobbily gook long enough.

Almost 80% of the world Jewish population live in Israel and the United States. With a population of 143 million less than 200,500 thousand live in Russia. With a population of 1.35 billion it will be hard to find more than 200 hundred in China, and at least 90% of those are lending some kind of technical support to the regime. So what are we missing here? If communism is so wonderful, why are we not living in these places where communism thrives? I would allow the intellectuals another paragraph to explain the dichotomy. Would you say the weather is to blame? Let me be the first

to admit to Russia's frozen tundra's and "epiphany frost".
But, here of late, Moscow has been warmer than the city of
New York, where almost 1.4 million Jewish Americans live.
In all honesty, what's a little cold weather when you're living
in a marxist paradise?   China has five temperature zones, and
just like the United States, it has high highs and low lows.
Cuba has perfect tropical weather year round, and is the most
marxist-leninist state we know, with the brothers Castro in
charge.   It's a "worker's paradise," if there ever was one.
The annual per capital income they say is almost $10,000 a
year.   But, we know it's probably closer to the Chinese,
which tops out at about $3,200 for college graduates. With a
population of 11 million people you might think its Jewish
population would be more than .007 of one percent.   I mean
if we are having all of this utopian fantasy over communism,
just the plane ride, or inner tube float over should make one
gitty with anticipation.   One should invite friends and family
to join them.   One shouldn't want all of this utopian paradise
all to themselves.

NO TAKERS: OSWALD'S ODD/DYSSEY:

Strangely, there's no takers. Especially, amongst liberal
professors who push this utopian crap on young people trying
to get through whatever high school or college course needed
to graduate.   At least, presidential assassin Lee Harvey
Oswald, had enough belief in marxism to put his life where
his mouth was. Soon after getting a discharge from the Marine
Corp, where he had been for nearly three years, the New
Orleans, native left America headed for Moscow, on his

utopian quest in September of 1959, with $1,700 dollars in his pocket. Mrs. Lincoln, or I should say Mrs. Kennedy, what about that play? At age nineteen young Harvey, said that "…he had read Soviet people lived good useful and very peaceful lives." This odd-ball had the gumption to act on the non-sense he had read, much less wrote. You would think the "intellectuals" who write or peddle this trife would act on it. There are those drug dealers who use their own product. But, these think it more important to hold down a wine glass filled with wine at some upper east side elitist soiree, than being total hypocrites.

     With visa running out, Oswald went as far as feigning suicide to remain and receive asylum in Russia. Now that's a hail Mary pass if there ever was one. Are there any takers in the ranks of the elitist intellectuals? Of course not. In light of the destruction marxist have brought on this country, you kind of have to give ol' Lee, a momentary pass on that whole Dealy Plaza, thing. Well, just long enough to admire his giant size rubles. I can almost look pass him offering up damaging military secrets in order to stay in Russia. Thank God there were no takers. The KGB didn't think no one in America would trust a lunatic like Lee Harvey Oswald, with vital national secrets. They don't know us that well. We elected a president suffering with the same abandonment ghost Oswald did. Distressed over family life back home, young Alek, settled into his new life in Minsk, with a 70 ruble a month subsidy from the Russian Red Cross, and a job at an "experimental shop" making radio and television parts. Soon thereafter, he became increasingly paranoid with the KGB's 24/7 surveillance of his life. They believed him to be a spy. Why else would someone leave America to live in

Russia?   He tore up his apartment once searching for listening devices.

Peter Savodnik, of the Wall Street Journal, said that: "Cold war Russians were usually lonely, wondering dislodged souls," During his odyssey, Oswald began to discover that the Russian people were every bit disjointed about their lives as he was his in America.   Russia was the "proper country" for his atheistic political views and a "dream" compared to the "decadent capitalistic society where workers are slaves."   As always the truth didn't live up to the hype.   Then, there's only one truth that lives up to the hype, and that's Jesus Christ, only He can cure the lonely, wondering dislodged soul.

Delusioned over the communist experiment and its utopian ruse, Oswald petition the Russian regime for permission to come back to the "decadent capitalist" society where "workers are slaves."   In part, the Russians had bent over backwards to accommodate Oswald.   They once thought to use him as some propaganda tool but thought better of it.   Oswald to them was an oddball that stuck out even in a bag of marbles.   After a year, he was granted permission to leave.   They hoped he had the time of his life, but, bidded him good riddance.   I am sure they realized he wasn't worth the bother.   The KGB believed American defectors to be "erratic" and "unstable."   Oswald, they thought to be "lazy" and "whiny."   So in June 1962 with Russian wife Marina and baby June Lee in tow, he arrived back into America with his hunt for Red Utopia over, the odyssey begun was now over; and the rest is nothing but history.   Still, Alek had the conviction to do what 99.99% of marxist intellectuals in the west will never do, and thats suspend hypocrisy long enough to go live in a communist country. That's why they are called arm chair revolutionaries by neo-conservatives. Proposing solutions for others they will never propose for themselves. For them it's a lot more courageous and stylish to bash America and capitalism from within, while laid back in an easy chair recliner sipping adult beverages.   At the same time, these oddest of oddballs, with champaign glasses in hand, denounce America's "decadent" opulence and toast its end as we know it.

HURRY BOYS:

Since slaves were first brought to New Amsterdam (New York), back in 1676, by the Dutch West India Company, there has been talk of Black people returning to Africa.   The so-called "colonization" of freed slaves began in earnest in 1817 with the American Colonization Society.   It's founding members wanted to help finance voyages for freed slaves back to places like Haiti, and the African countries of Siberia, and Sierra Leone.   There were some takers. Abraham Lincoln, had become a supporter of the ACS in the 1840's.   Later, he believed it to be a way to overcome the obstacles of ending slavery.   But, friend of Lincoln, former slave Frederick Douglas, called it a "red herring."   In 1849 Douglas wrote in his newspaper "The North Star," that it was a "ruse to divert the attention of the people from the foul abomination which is sought to be forced upon the free soul of "some states".   Still, his good friend whom he called a "great man," thought that "racial harmony" was unachievable in the United States.   Lincoln believed colonization with some combination of "emancipated compensation" would go a long way toward making the Emancipation Proclamation, more palatable to southern Democrats and slave-owners. Eventually, Lincoln agreed with Douglas, and went full blow about ending slavery.

Since its inception in Detroit, Michigan, in the 1930's, the Nation of Islam, has been the focal point of the Black separatist movement. Leaders like Louis Farrakhan, (affectionately known as "Calyso Louie" on talk radio) has messaged on a 51 state solution. Farrakhan, feels that Blacks are owed a state of their own because of their contributions to America. He said if conditions like "full and complete freedom," "equal justice" and "equal membership in society" are not met then "separation would be the solution to our race problem." I have always thought that words like "justice" and "freedom" coming out of a so-called civil rights leader's mouth were empty words filled with a lot of sound good. Nevertheless, nowhere in his proclamations does the good minister mention going back to Africa. His separation rhetoric stops at shores end.

Over the years, there have been those civil rights leaders that have called for a return to Africa by Black people. They've rehearsed the now tired language of America being a racist country with the "mans" foot on every Black person's neck for decades now. Most would agree, America has had its racial components, but no other country in the history of the world has done more to rectify its racial discord. It is the race hustlers, egged on by white Democrats, who continuously fan these flames of racism because it brings them attention, fame, and money. Thus, it's more of a hustle than a clarion call, this foot on neck nonsense has paralyze far too many Blacks into not striving to be all they can be, in spite of racism.

For other Black radicals, their solution was for us Black folks to go back to Africa; as if they wanted us there contaminating their gene pool. Forget the nightmare logistics of it all. Anyhoo, I remember going to a lecture that turned into a rally, held by the late Stokely Carmichael (Kwame Ture), in the late 1970's on the campus of Texas Southern University. Carmichael's speech was the usual America is racist rant. But, he added a unique twist. He said because of it we Black folks should go back to Africa. I believe he use the word "imperative" several times. Being young naive, and impressionable, I was sold! What the F—K!" I said to myself in an arena filled with other Black kids like myself screaming to the top of their lungs "back to Africa!" "back to Africa!" I was ready to get back to my dorm room and call my dad to get money for airfare to whatever African nation. He would have gladly sprung for a one way ticket.

I had always been somewhat of a separatist. My mother and father didn't believe in desegregation. They taught us that Black folks should be with Black folks; and White folks should be with White folks. My mother even warned against marrying a Catholic girl. I went to an all-Black elementary school; an all Black high school, and an predominately Black college. I grew up in an all Black part of town. I could never understand why civil right leaders were always talking about desegregation this and desegregation that. I have met a lot of extremely nice White people in my life. Of course, we all have our pretenders present when we're in public, but I know when people are faking it. Still, I have never had a White friend. The questions I ask as I look in the mirror, is whether this has been a subconscious design, or the unluckiness of the draw.

NOTE: If you ask a Rush Limbaugh, how many Black friends he has had in his life; no doubt he would count all ten fingers and toes before he finished counting them. I am not sure if Rush has had any other race of friend. Similar things can be said about Sean Hannity, and other conservatives. On the other hand, nothing of the sort could be said about Washington D.C. liberals. If someone called for a "bring your Black friend to work day" more than 90% of these elites would have to call a White friend and ask if they knew an African American person. A lot of maids, yard men, and limo drivers would suddenly find out they had White BFF's that they were not aware of until that day, and only for that day. Otherwise Barak Obama, and Al Roker, will be very busy on bring your Black friend to work day. Bill Clinton, once called Obama a porter. That's how White liberal elites see us, nothing more than their servants or slaves.

In my arrogance and ignorance, I thought White people weren't good enough to be in the company of Black people. That's not what my parents taught me, but it's what I grew to believe. I never considered myself a racist, just someone who believed in the doctrine of separate but equal. I never was a big fan of Brown v. Board of Education. It was the beginning of the end for Black schools. Just like Jackie Robinson's move to the Major Leagues in 1947 was the end of the Negro League. At that time in my life I couldn't get my mini mind around why the "castaways" wanted off Gilligan's Island. All that separation from the world. How cool is that?

After walking out of the Stokely Carmichael, "back to Africa" rally, other than some native Africans, I was the only non "original" Black still jazzed and pumped from the speech. With overwhelming excitement I ask a few folk, including friends, how soon will they be leaving for Africa? To the man, and woman, they all said: I am not from Africa; I don't know nobody in Africa; and I am not going to Africa. There would be no twelve thirty flights. I thought…but…, what the…., weren't you one of the ones screaming: back to Africa? He said it was "imperative" that we leave soon. It turns out it was just for the moment. In retrospect, it now reminds me of church folk who shout and amen everything the preacher says with no intentions of doing a word of it. Just like then and now, there were no takers. Hurry boys she's waiting there for you, fell on realistic ears itching for a quick thrill longing for some solitary company. Not a few White people have quietly recommended, after hearing the incessant rants of racism a return to the Motherland by Black people. I myself, have openly and repeatedly suggested the same. I know of no takers. With all the supposed racism in America, you would think they couldn't wait to bless the rains down in Africa, and hear wild dogs cry out in the night. Apparently, it's going to take a lot to drag them away from here. I can take the time to do the things I never had right here in America. And it's going to take a "million" men or more to make me leave.

Lee Harvey Oswald, for a moment in time, let the courage of his convictions carry him away to a distant land. The race hustlers, both Black and White, and the "Hate America First," crowd loves to bash her for all of her insignificant faults.   But, those nothings unlike Oswald are in no hurry to take us up on our offer and leave. They will never hurry away from here. They will never take us up on our offer and leave.

GET OVER IT!:

Nobel Peace Prize laureate Milton Freidman (1912-2006), said that Jews owe an enormous debt to free enterprise and competitive capitalism.   He believed Jews thrive the most in a free deregulated capitalist society.   Yet, for at least the last past century and a half they have consistently been opposed to capitalism.   He called it a "paradox." Juxtaposing West Germany and East Germany, Friedman wrote, "…both have people of the same blood, they are the same civilization with the same technical skills and knowledge torn asunder by war; separated by a wall.   One adopts a social market economy, the other a central planning one." Fast forward a few years later, and the black and white of its communist versus capitalism glares loudly.   Friedman then ask: "which side of the wall is there tyranny and misery, and on which side of the wall is there "freedom and affluence?"

One side of the wall built the wall in order to keep its people from escaping.   While cold hard facts and reality does not impress nor change the minds of many intellectuals, I ask, if collectivisms is paradise, why the need to build walls, install land mines and erect barbed wire fences, complete with guard post and guard dogs to keep people in? Freedom loving people have risked life and limb to escape communist China, Russia, Cuba, and East Germany and other collectivist states. My grasp on reality tells me nobody tries to escape paradise. Whenever Jews have been allowed to leave Russia they do en-masse. They ask no questions non-other than: "how fast can we leave? No one begs to stay. Another paragraph for intellectual elites is to explain this paradox. Why do people risk their lives to escape a place arm chair revolutionaries deem paradise?

Friedman was stomped by this dichotomy of Jews benefitting enormously from capitalisms yet hating it. In his book, "Why Jews Should Not be Liberal." Larry F. Sternberg, boils it down to misinterpretation of terms and words. Sternberg says, during the mass exodus from under Alexander's III, tyranny in the early 1880's, Jews that fled were said to be following the "liberal cause" which was to "liberate" them from the ghettos. Thus, "liberal" became a heroic term. During this time socialism was the doctrine most often preached as the way to a better life. He says that most Jews that accepted socialism were not aware of its dictionary definition, which was "control by the state of all means of production and economic activity." He goes on to say that socialism's veneer of "Brotherhood, Charity and Sharing" was appealing. That's why the Nazis incorporated it into their National Socialist Party banner; and the communist labeled themselves the International Socialist Movement.

Elie Kedourie, discusses in his book "The Jewish

World," that American Jews have long believed that ignorance of social problems of poverty, prejudice and practices of discrimination against Jews were inventions of the right.   But, here in later years Jews are starting to discover that many Jewish problems emanate from the left.   In its "affluence," "permissiveness" and "wishful thinking" it has "substituted" liberalism for Judaism.   His books critique goes onto say, what American Jews must always remember is that "totalitarianism regimes come to power by promising everything to everybody, and then remain in power through force and "intimidation."

Rabbi Byron L. Sherwin (Faith Finding Meaning: A Theology of Judaism) said in a Front Page magazine interview, that at the turn of World War II Jewish immigrants in America were suffering "widespread social and economic discrimination, rampart anti-semitism, poverty, lack of employment opportunities, political marginalization, a feeling of vulnerability, and a perception that conservatives considered Jews as personas non grata in America."   All reminiscent of what happen to them in Europe – propelled Jewish immigrants and their children into the liberal and radical camps.   Rabbi Sherwin, said that American Jews perception of the Roosevelt administration – its advocacy of "government activism" in support of economic growth; its support of unions, the poor and middle class workers, and the opportunities of government service afforded to Jews and others to be in their best interest.   Excuse me, but wasn't this kind of government or regime heavy handed meddling in the lives of people is what drove them from Europe.   If anybody or any immigrant group that should have been suspect of this level of government involvement it should have been Jews.

While all of this government "activism" sounds good, and may feel good. It might be good for a while – the end result or end game has always been financial collapse and/or a state of dictatorial rule.

While Jews have nobody to blame for their success but themselves, Roosevelt's New Deal policies marked the beginning of the decimation of the Black Family and its ability to formulate capital to compete in a national and global economy. We were told to just lie back and let the government take care of it until this day, the government hasn't took care of it. It wasn't the god of liberalism nor did Johnson's societal planning that propel Jews into upper financial stratums. It was the American free enterprise and endeavor system that allowed them to use their God given abilities to set and accomplish any goal they set for themselves without government interference. Roosevelt and his New Deal, didn't have a doggone thing to do with it. At best, it only hindered efforts to make one's life achievement goals harder.

Roosevelt wouldn't even allow the MS St Louis ocean liner, which had almost a thousand German Jew refugees aboard it to dock here in the United States in the late 1930"s. Jewish apologist for Roosevelt have excused him by blaming the League of Nations, Congress, other countries and the American people. Roosevelt attracters, claim he had this grand plan of spending 150 million dollars to save some 20,000 Jews from war torn Europe, and disburse them amongst the U.S. and other countries where maybe off chance that this was true. But in the context of 20,000 Jews, the near one thousand aboard the MS St Louis represented only 5 percent of that figure and wouldn't have cost the American taxpayer a dime despite American anti-semitism or congressional foot dragging, to the contrary, Roosevelt, could have wheeled his executive order or amnesty pen and allowed the ocean liner to dock here in safe harbors. If Roosevelt was facing any political pressure not to allow the docking, it was from within his own Democrat party, and not from Republicans. Since when has a Democrat cared about anything a Republican thinks? The MS St Louis, seemingly limped back on to Europe shores where almost 200 of its passengers died in concentration camps. No one is claiming Roosevelt to be anti-semitic, he just did what any good Democrat would do when given the chance, and that's screw you. Democrats are very adept at slippery soap in prison shower opportunities.

Further into the interview, the Rabbi said, Jews are not scared off by the rising anti-semitism in the Democrat party. He says "Jews much prefer the anti-Israel proclivities of the left to the pro-Israel positions of the right." So it is that Jewish intellectuals bend over backwards and prison shower forward to make Democrat Franklin Delano Roosevelt, out to be some Jewish Messiah, and Republican President Richard M. Nixon, some sort of Barabbas. While Jewish intellectuals like the late Marvin Kalb, thought he was the most anti-semitic person since Hitler, - Israeli Jews see him as a hero. Nixon did more for the Jewish state than Roosevelt ever could have imagine. With the operation Nickel Grass arms lift doing the Yom Kippur war, (October 1973) Nixon order with a sense of urgency the resupply of military weapons and hardware to the Jewish state. The Israeli army was then able to take back land lost to the overwhelming military forces of the Syrian and Egyptian armies. They were supplied by "communist" Russia. Nixon didn't go to the United Nations or consult congress, nor hide behind the American people. He took charge and did what needed to be done. In human parlance, Israel owes its existence to him. While Roosevelt, was an excellent "D" Day planner, he was late on the draw with the Holocaust and its Auschwitzes. Jewish Democrats would rather spend an hour in a crematorium oven than admit to that.

Rabbi Sherwin, said that Jews have a "fear," "mistrust" and "prejudice" against many Christian institutions and their spokespersons. No doubt, there has been antagonism between Christian and Jews since the 1st century A.D. For more than two and a half centuries Christians were persecuted by the "Imperial Cult" or Roman state under emperors such as Augustus and Nero, along with Jews and other "baser sorts." It wasn't until the beginning of the 4th Century when Emperor Constantine I, with his "Edict of Milan" made Christianity legal in the Roman Empire. His Christian mother influenced him to. This not only made Jews mad, but made Judaism, illegal. Jews were forced to convert to Christianity or leave Roman providences. Fast forward to the end of the 4th Century with Pope Urban II blessings, began a two hundred year campaign to rid the Holy Land of Islamic rule and allow Christianity access. Certainly, Jews were caught in the crossfire and thousands of them were killed. But no case can be made that the Jews were a ethnic or religious target per see' of what we know as the "Crusades." Still, historians may disagree. Jews even today hold on to it as though it happen yesterday, as a reason for distrusting Christianity and Christians.

In the last one and a half centuries there has been a lot of persecution of Jews by supposed Christian states and priest. Especially doing the Tsarist age of Russia. It wasn't until Joseph Stalin, aligned anti-semitism to "cannibalism" that altitudes may have begun to change. Prior to that, at the turn of the 19th century, the Russian Orthodox Church had begun to take steps to quail anti-semitism amongst its members. Even with all of its antagonism of Jews, through the centuries, as a body count, it's not even negligible compared to socialism and communism's decimation of the Jewish race and culture. Besides, nowhere in Christian literature does it allow for persecution of Jews on the basis of ethnicity or religion. In fact, Christians are told by God to bless Abraham's seeds. When someone steps outside that commandment their Christianity or adherence to God's statutes should be questioned. Moreover, Jews should know better than anyone, for the actions of a few being blamed on the whole. It's cynical beyond cynicism to allow what happen centuries ago to hunt your mind as a make believe to assassinate Christianity. I stand to brag that the overwhelming majority of the 24,336 members on the Holocaust Memorial's "Righteous amongst the Nations" list were Christians. No doubt, a lot of Jews support Christian television financially. But Jews en-masse must recognize the only friends they have left in the world, whether orthodox or secular, are Christians and conservatives. Especially, the John Hagee, Rush Limbaugh, and Glen Beck, wings of both. These plead your case when the marxist media refuse to. Columnist George Will, ask some anti-school prayer Rabbi, if they were walking down the street late at night in a rough neighborhood and three Black men emerged out of a building would they prefer the men to be leaving a party or a Bible study? So it's time for Jews to get over whatever consternation they have held for Christianity these thousands of years.   My personal explanation for why Jews don't like capitalism is that they equate it with Christianity.   That being the case, capitalism has been good to Jews so has Christianity. Therefore, it is time to get over it.

SAY GOOD BYE TO ALL THAT:

Conservative author and lecturer David Horowitz, and colleague Peter Collier, came out of the closet in a 1985 Washington Post, article entitled "Goodbye to All That." While their "coming out" wasn't met with the same fanfare as a Ellen DeGeneres, or the latest sexually perverted athlete, complete with atta boys, or atta girls---, or ---whatever (it gets confusing) from the president and first lady, nonetheless, it was a stunning availing.   Both Horowitz and Collier admitted to...to...to...voting for Ronald Reagan.   These two born bred and raised marxist voted for the most conservative and anti-marxist president ever.

Horowitz, parents were avowed members of the communist party USA, but became dissolution with its idealism when Russian Nikita Khrushev, gave his so-called "secret speech."   Khrushev was deeply critical of the former dictator Joseph "The man of steel" Stalin, by calling his mortified body out on the Kremlin carpet in February of 1956 for his brutal purges and murder sprees.   So his parents became disillusioned and broke with the communist party. As a side note, I have to ask, why didn't they already know about Stalin's atrocities?   Anyhoo, young David went on to become a known quantity in marxist circles.   He and Collier became editors of a leftist publication called "Rampart." They were on speaking terms with terrorist Bill Ayers, and his Weather Underground; and raised money for the marxist organization "The Black Panthers."   It wasn't until Horowitz recommended to the Black Panthers, that they hire a Betty Van Potter, as their bookkeeper.   She ended up floating in the San Francisco harbor in December of 1974.   Even though no one was ever arrested for the murder, Horowitz was certain it was at the hands of the Black Panther's leadership.   She was known to raise questions about financial irregularities.

What Horowitz and Collier were saying goodbye to were the personality facets that come to be known as "the hate America first crowd" that combinated during the Vietnam War.   They wrote that these were "self aggrandizing" with a "romance" for corrupt "third worldism" with a casual indulgence of Soviet Totalitarianism" along with "self dramatizing anti-Americanism."   Horowitz, use the word "hypocritical" when describing American marxist.   The phrase "American marixist" use to be an oxy-moron, now it's becoming more redundant. "Hypocritical," in my opinion, is putting a positive spin on who these imps are. When you judge them in light of the bloodshed their actions have caused, there are no lexiconian apps available to plug-in.   The adjectives have not yet been invented that would adequately describe these monsters.   During the Viet Nam war, imps like Bill Clinton, allowed themselves to be used as useful idiots by North Vietnamese communist dictator Ho Ching Menh.   In their incessant protest of the American war efforts, the war was ruled "unwinnable" by Walter Cronkite.   In the interim, President Johnson allowed American soldiers to languish (in the late sixties' early seventies') in the Vietnam jungles without much logistical support. Once President Nixon, brought them home, the South Vietnamese were left to fend for themselves. Between the Russian backed North Vietnamese and Cambodian communist dictator Polpot and his Khmer Rouge, millions of East Asians were slaughtered. American arm chair marxist like "The Nation" excused the murders as necessary to …, "restore some semblance of civilized government" to the devastated countries; and calling the genocidal blood bath a "rescue mission." To compound this absurdity, American marxist blamed America for the bloodshed because our government refused to normalize relations with the newly formed cadre of murderous thugs.

Again, the words have not yet been invented that would describe these animals. "Self-aggrandizing" and "self-dramatizing" should be considered compliments for these monsters enlight of the genocide their lives and actions have caused. Cold, callous, and other than red hot hatred for America and its populace, these arm chair murderers are emotionally dead. During the Gulf War (1990 ,1991), under George Bush these dogs of war tried to relive their glory days.

The end of the Vietnam war left the marxist movement with nothing to do and in somewhat of a depressive state. It was their heyday moment, now it was gone. Horowitz wrote some felt "a sense of emptiness." So they attach themselves to murdering communist dictators around the world in the form of cheerleaders such as Kim Il Jong of North Korea, and Mengistu of Ethiopia. Together with cheshire grins these demons watch millions of their people die of starvation. Stalin taught them well. In the meantime Kim and Mengistu lived lavished lives, the same imperialist arrangement marxist claim they hate. Frauds all! Sic Semper tyrannis.

In times past these degenerates held protest and rallies outside the halls of power, like Bill Clinton, Hillary Clinton, and Barak Obama.   Now their positions have changed, and they are now the power they once hated.   Their positions have changed, but their marxist "romance" has only grown. But, those like Horowitz and Collier, have said goodbye to their marxist romance.   It's time all of America say goodbye to the marxist that make up the Democrat Party.   When we do that, we say bye to the systematic dismantling of our country as we know it – we say bye to uncontrollable deficits – we say goodbye to the mass genocide of unborn children – we say bye to our drift toward deeper serfdom – we say bye to the systematic decimation of the Black family – we say goodbye to high crime rates – we say goodbye to a lot of racial antagonism – we say goodbye to the overwhelming inflation in food and gas prices – we say bye to failing schools.   The list of evils we say bye to is endless when we stop voting for Democrats.   We should be glad to say goodbye to all that.

Now we begin to pull ourselves out of the dundrums of a communist tilt.   Obama says we might as well get used to it, **"NO WE WON'T!"** There will be no more c'est la vie, que sera sera, or that's just the way it is, things will never change. As marxist Bill Clinton, would say "we have to have the courage to change."   Not his kind of change, but that given of God.

EPITAPH:

As always, when we say bye to one thing we have to say hello to another, or we end up going back to that thing that had us in bondage.   We cannot arrive at one destination without leaving another.   When someone quit smoking cigarettes, it is recommended that they develop another oral fixation.   Preferably, one much more healthier.   When we say goodbye to Democrats, we must take a momentary pause to inquire within ourselves why is it we voted for them in the first place?   The Democrats are very skillful at portraying themselves as caring people.   Their vagrant consciences allows them to tell us any lie they think we want to hear; aided by an equally scrupleless media that helps them convince us. The Bible says satan comes as an "angel of light." That's what these imps do, they brilliance us with glowing empty platitudes of caring and understanding our every need. But, their hearts are far from any concern for anybody; power and the abuse of it is all they are concern with.   Many are seduced with these empty words because it makes them feel someone understands and cares for them.   Like the moth they are drawn to the flame of platitudinous words. We all must examine our motives.   Maybe you are cold and callous person who likes the devastation being reeked on America by Democrats.   Then maybe you are a person that likes the permissiveness and promiscuous life style Democrats promote, and you don't want to be judged for your own depravity.   So they make you feel comfortable in your own skin and sin. Everyone who votes for Democrats has to examine themselves as to why.   There is no sane reason to vote for Democrats.   When we make our break from them we have to examine those demons within that hold us captive to their excessive flaws and failures.   Why were we birds of a feather?   From there we can move on to the truth about liberals and their politics and never return; we want get fooled again.   Democrats are very adept at appealing to our lower nature.   They spend billions of dollars along with billions of propaganda dollars in free favorable publicity from the marxist media to further the lie that Republicans, are rich fat cats; the scum of the universe, racist misogynist pigs, who can't be trusted with the reins of power.   When in fact, it's Democrats (who are rich fat cats…the scum of the universe, racist misogynist pigs) that can't be trusted with the reins of power.   This isn't propaganda, its documented fact.

In the grand scheme of it all, turning away from the lies and destruction of the Democrats is nary a bit part in it all. As an individual, the paradox of calling ourselves Christian and acting like anything but one.   The same for the nation. Calling America a Christian nation and, like Bible Babylon, it has become the most hedonistic place on earth.   We must now reconcile the two extremes.   There must be a wholesale, both corporate and individually review of our sins.   We must look at how far we have fallen from that high mark of One Nation under God.   And not make excuses and blame others. We need to visit the nearest mirror.   If we'll going to turn from unscrupulous politicians we must turn back to God, through His Son Jesus Christ, individually and collectively. Then we find morally sound "born again" people to represent us in government.   The Bible says, "when the righteous are in charge the people rejoice."   But when a wicked man rules, the people groan (NKJV).   Can you hear America groaning, maybe never like you've heard in its history?   Righteousness exalts a nation but sin is a reproach to a people.   Because of the darkness in our own hearts we cleave to ourselves teachers and politicians with equally dark wicked hearts.   We are not the Democrat party, they are us.   They simply took our depravity and added to it. We find ourselves and our nation upon this precipice, do we corporately and individually continue down the same road that have destroyed empires (Babylonian, Roman, Russian, etc.) before ours or do we on this day choose whom we will serve satan or God. I highly, highly recommend God. When we fail to make a conscious effort to repent of our sins and ask Jesus Christ, to come into our lives save and make us one of his children by giving us His Holy Ghost, then we have by default and automatically given ourselves over to satan. Who needs that?

Query: Was it Bill Clinton's repeat acts of adultery that drew you to him? Is it Barak Obama's hate for America that has drawn you to him? Is it Mick Romney's, decency that causes you to be repulsed by him? Crackheads, homosexuals, bad kids, etc., are attracted to each other without first knowing the moral makeup up of the other. Crackheads spirits automatically connect to other crackheads. So it is with all sinful behavior. This time, polar negatives attract. If you are attracted to a sleeze-ball politician, chances are you are a sleeze-ball person. Personalities and colors of their skin or dress tie should never be a reason for voting for or against them. We should look at their content of character.

The problem with America isn't global warming as the leftist in government, academia, and the media would have us believe, that's not causing the climatic woes, sin is. Has anyone ever read the sixth chapter of Genesis? Sin only feels good for a minute, but its consequences can last a lifetime, or be the direct result of a short life. For the wages of sin is death (First, a spiritual death then a physical one) God, stands ready to welcome us with open arms and forgive us our sins, if we ask.

I want my fourscore and seven plus years to stand for something positive.   In my twilights, I want to look back and see the good that God wrought through me.   I want to be able to look back at all those people lives I had a positive effect on. Even if it only was a kind word or a kind smile at a critical time in their lives.   Lord knows, others have done it for me. I want to see, in my mind's eye, the drug addict that's now free from drugs; the homosexual that's now married with children, free from the guilt and shame of his perversion.   I want to have been involved in another "Great Awakening" in America, where we as a nation cry out to God, and ask Him to restore America to its rightful place in Him: and we repent, forsake our sins, ourselves and our idol gods of sex, greed, and selfishness.   I have always believed that a man's life should be geared toward leaving a legacy where people would be glad that he was once in the earth because of the affect he had on them.   I often ask myself what would that dash between the year I was born and the year I passed on my gravestone say about my time here on earth.   I cry sometimes because I might not live up to the legacy my mother and father left here.   But, God knows.   There is no greater life than living yours for others.   Not becoming their doormat, but taking the time to be there for them.   Even when it's most inconvenient for you.   The most miserable people on earth are selfish ones.   These are the ones who make the pharmaceutical companies and psychiatrist richer.   They are always taking something to make them happy; or asking someone, why am I not happy?   The purpose driven life is taking care of God's business and God's business is people. When you get your mind on other people, not their faults and short comings, but their needs; then you forget about yours. In the meantime God is taking care of yours. It's not your job to take on the world, just that piece of it that God gives you. He knows exactly what He made you for. He knows your perfect fit. That thing or problem you are attracted to because you want to solve it, might be it. If it brings you joy and energy in addition to heartache and pain than that's it. In the end we all should do the work of an evangelist. Every Christian should take it upon themselves to tell someone about the love of Jesus Christ and His saving grace. This is my greatest passion. Every Christian should be willing to inconvenience themselves to do it. Evangelism is imperative.

It has always confused me, maybe even bothered me, why people like Joseph Stalin, Adolf Hitler, and Mao Zedong, would want to heave as much misery and destruction on mankind as humanly possible, before assuming room temperature (dying: for those of you in Rio Linda). What led them to believe they would live forever and not have to face their maker? The "enlightens" don't believe in a devil that blinds their eyes to his existence. Intellectuals can't phantom the evil spirit that guides them. For it is appointed once for man to die and after that the judgment. Every knee shall bow, and every tongue will confess and give an account of himself to God. We all will stand before the judgment seat of God, and will need a good lawyer to plead our case. In fact, we will need the perfect lawyer and there's only one that graduated cum laude from the law school of Death, Burial and Resurrection and that's esquire Jesus Christ. He sits on the right hand of God and pleads our case. He has never lost a case.   Once we receive His blood as atonement for our sins, He becomes our attorney.   And we are found innocent of all charges and pass on to heaven when we pass on.   No matter how perfect a life we may think we may have led, we all will need Jesus as our advocate.   The law firm of Clinton, Clinton and Obama won't get it done.   They will be too busy explaining their miserable lives and the havoc they desired to wreak on the United States and its people.   These momma or daddy issue folk are like that.   Global warming will be an "epiphany frost" compared to where they're going if they don't repent. Then again, they may want to visit some old mentor or idol. It's insane to want to heap destruction on anyone.   It is downright demonic.   We all should want to leave the world in better shape than we found it, these don't.

I believe a large part of America's spiritual renewal largely depends on the way we treat Israel.   God says in the 12th chapter of Genesis that, "Those that bless Israel will be blessed and those that curse her I will curse."   America has experienced its prosperity largely because it has been a blessing to the nation of Israel being the first country to recognize it as a sovereign state May 14, 1948 at 6:00 PM eastern standard time.   Other countries with the exception of leaders are cursed because of the way they have treated Israel; history bares it out.   With a reluctance by Israel leaders to acquiesce and give the West Bank and the Gaza Strip over to the PLO terrorist front without any concession, thus, making it completely surrounded outside and inside by its sworn enemies and world leftist. This also includes those in the United States that are increasingly becoming openly perturbed and hostile toward the Jewish state across the nations.   In an effort to appease Obama, and his leftist conspirators, the Democrat party, with Jewish campaign money in pocket and Jewish votes in hand, refused to call Jerusalem, the capital of Israel, in its party's platform. In its grand plan to kick Black folks to the proverbial curb once illegal alien votes can be counted, they pose the same desertion and piss-off of Jews when Islamic money (OPEC) and votes become more available. Remember, Hitler, co-conspirator and good friend of the Mufti, called both Blacks and Jews monkeys. Then, now, does the conundrum clouds clear. Democrats not only hate Blacks, they hate Jews too. With the skies clear and the myth disproved will Jewish people and leaders on both sides of the Mediterranean continue to hide their heads up their asses and still imagine Democrats, and socialist are their friends and protectors? Will being a "good" Democrat continue to be at the top of their bucket list, and just above the Star of David on their gravestones? That and a dollar want buy you a fifty cent cup of coffee. This is a worthless and sorry ass epitaph to work toward (pardon my yiddish). So far, Black folk hadn't woken up to the targets Democrats have placed on their backs either.

Both communities have shared a deep rich parallel history. Both have a history of slavery and shared a deep love and dependence on God. One is hated by the atheist strut of the Democrat party for its chosen of God status; the other because it no longer endures forced slavery. Both relegated to ghettos by their enemy, the Jews by Russians Czars and the Nazi party; Black folk by themselves and the Democrat Party. Both protected from their enemies by God. Black folk think they have a monopoly on persecution and racism, but its nil compared to that Jews have suffered. Other than Democrats, no one has ever wanted us exterminated. Now it's time for one to return to that dependency on God and the other to finally en-masse, accept that Yeshua Jesus is Messiah. They need to stop blaming God for the Holocaust, and all the other awful things that's happen. When we reject Jesus Christ, we automatically reject God. Jesus is the way and the truth and the life. No man gets to God accept by Him. Se we can't have one and not the other. With His death, burial and resurrection, we moved from the law into grace; from the Old Testament to the New Testament, from religion to relationship, from the old covenant to the new covenant. There's no more need for rituals, animal sacrifice, reciting the Ten Commandments, and observing days. These are no longer necessary as a means of reaching God. Jesus was the Lamb of God that took away the sins of the world. In Jesus, the Ten Commandments are written down in our hearts. When we are filled with His Holy Spirit, we have an umpire that guides us into to all truth. We no longer have to walk around with copies of the law or phylacteries. The only reform Judaism that needs to take place is the accepting of Jesus Christ. He came first to the Jew, then the Gentile.

Jesus is the answer to anti-semitism, racism and the two state bogosity. All of Israel and much of the Middle East where in five world capitols are has been promised to the Jews by God. And I believe Jesus holds the title deed ready to convey ownership to the Jews. And while it is this movement to recast Palestinians, as "Y" chromosomes Jews, they are Jordanians. Like Ariel Sharon said, "Let them give them a homeland." By God's survey markers, they have no right to one grain of sand belonging to Israel. Jordan is almost 4.5 times the size of Israel. Saudi Arabia, which is the biggest agitator of a Palestinians homeland inside Israel, is almost 95 times the size of Israel. Certainly, they can find some spare land to put them, they too are Arabs. It has nothing to do with a Palestinians homeland. It's a strategy to surround Israel both from within and without, and then they attack. Every time they've attacked from without, Israel kick ass and took names and territory (again, please pardon my yiddish). Instead of veni, vidi, vici, it has been veni, vidi, perdi. Translated into yiddish: we came, we saw, but they kicked our asses. Thank God, the paradigm hadn't awaken and the pogroms started. For a nation like Israel to give up the West Bank and the Gaza Strip to terrorist would be the same as a state of equal size Massachusetts, to give up everything south east of Lexington, and everything south west of Amherst. Let's see how the good politically correct folk in Massachusetts, like being squeezed in by well-armed Jihadist.

Bill Clinton, practically broke the arm of Israeli Prime Minister Ehud Barak, to make this deal with terrorist Yasser Arafat, who visited the White House more than Monica Lewinsky. My God! Bill, wanted that Nobel Peace Prize so bad, Israel giving up her security and sovereignty was such a small price to pay for his self-adulation and aggrandizement. Imagine his anger when Obama was awarded his just for showing up to work two days in a row. Not bad for a porter. That Nobel Peace Prize was to replace the cross on his gravestone. Arafat's Janazah and tombstone would have read: "I am the one who destroyed the Jewish state." It would have been all the talk down at the Casbah. For an Islamic terrorist, what better epitaph to have. Then again, peace with Israel and a two state solution resolution would have meant the end of the billions of dollars Arafat, was getting from world leaders to help the Palestinian people, in which he and his wife Suha pocketed almost all of it.   So he said no to the Camp David accords even though Clinton forced Barack to fork over Israel to the agent terrorist.   His epitaph should read the same as Jesse Jackson's and Al Sharpton's well maybe even WEB Dubois, "Here lies a so called leader who was in it all for himself."

THE ALINSKYITES:

Once Obama gets his tanks and pink army into position, a new order arises.   People who were cunned into becoming comfortable and at ease with others paying their way;   who were told those people in the Tea Party were mean because they wanted to take away their gravy train now are forced into labor camps at gunpoint by Obama's pink army thugs. They are made to work 20 plus hours a day.   They are given no union representation or food nor water.   Once they drop dead from exertion and starvation their bodies are toshed into a mass grave with the other dead dumbasses, who fell for the Alinsky styled psych-ops campaign.   For decades they bribed us with our own money, now they shoot us with our own guns. Whether Benjamin Franklin, or Alexander Tytler, the originor, still, the quote holds true. "A democracy cannot exist as a permanent form of government.   It can only exist until the majority discovers it can vote itself largess out of the public treasury". Karl Marx said it like this, "Communism could be brought about in a democratic society through legislative reform and peaceful means."   Apparently, the

Obama, Bill and Hillary Alinskyites want even have to fire a
shot to defeat and enslave us.   Alinskyites, Richard Cloward
and Frances Fox Pivens, both of ACORN, subprime crises,
and motor-voter laws, said that, "The strategy for forcing
political change should be through orchestrated crisis." They
believe by overloading the government bureaucracy with a
"flood of impossible demands," thus pushing society into
crisis and economic collapse, should hasten the fall of
capitalism.

At the same time the Alinskyites are working this angle
of our demise, marxist in the entertainment industry are
tearing away at our moral fiber.   Studio heads, directors,
writers, producers, and actors are at a 24/7 clip of non-stop
moral rot broadcasting filth as entertainment.   With a
hundred and fifty channels you can count on one hand the
shows and/or characters that may have a semblance of a moral
thread.   It's a 24/7 orgy of inconsequential sex scenes and
alludes.   It's all presented as one big ball of glamor. No one
can safely say they are not in some bit part affected by it.
Billions of soft drinks and other products have been sold with
scantily clad women; some with shirtless men.   Even bright
shining red racing cars somehow look better with a bikini clad
girl flung across its hood.   It's all designed in part to scrip
away our moral conscience.   We reason, it can't be that bad if
the "beautiful people" are doing it.   We tune into shows like
Entertainment Tonight, to catch up with what they are doing.
There are never no judgments made concerning their aberrant
behavior.   Even when they go way off the deep end, it's met
with a "well you know," smile by the brain dead host.   I am
convinced a pretty smile and an empty head is all that's
required to get one of these gigs.   People with moral

absolutes need not apply.   We are told with straight faces, that an actress that got married that Friday is now pregnant by and marrying another actor that Monday, of sorts.   It's all made to look glamorous, no matter how bad it is.

Once they strip away your moral construct, owning your heart and mind becomes easy.   Nationalism becomes obsolete, and now you are a puppet on a string, subject to their whims.   They tell you who to hate.   They tell you who to love.   They tell you bad is good and good is evil.   What was up is now down.   What was wrong is now right.   With their "social English" and "Newspeak" you find yourself in Winston Smith's nightmare.   Without a moral compass or a 1+1=2 foundation, you believe and do what they tell you to. They tell you freedom is bad and communism is good, you believe it.   They tell you capitalism is bad but communism is good, you believe it.   Hollywood has helped the Alinskyites in bringing this degree of mind numbity about.   Big Brother, wants to lull us into this moral desertion.   Neo marxist Saul Alinsky knew something that Karl Marx didn't.   That is communism is an unworkable economic theory, that want bring the quasi-utopia theorized it would.   It has only brought the dystopia of almost a hundred million people dying from murder, starvation and disease.   While the communist central committee members looked on from their palatial estates or palaces with unemotional glee, while they and the ruling class benefit financially from the things produced through gun point diplomacy.   A quick peek at history then and now, proves me out.

NOTE: The only thing more deadly than communism is

Islam. It's historical death count outpaced communism. Only thing, the mullahs are much more anxious to kill than allow time for disease or starvation to do it. The Koran does allow for slavery, but who has time for that? They figure the cave don't need sweeping. There's no dry cleaning that needs to be picked up. So "I kill you", and enjoy the buzz of bloodletting, do the mullah yell, and move on to the next victim. The Koran says it's alright to kill the infidel, but leave his wife and children alone. Yeah right!" You think these animals are going to slit the throat of the head of household and leave his wife and 2.4 kids intact, hah!" You don't kill 240 million people obeying the Koran. Killing has no holiday with these yahoos. There is no rhyme or reason why they kill. They don't need occasion just opportunity. The marxist media still try to tell us that they have legitimate reasons or gripes for their murderous protest. No, they don't. It's no more than their vampirish need to see blood dripping from someone's slit throat. It's their crack cocaine. These are Chaldeans. They don't regard silver or gold. The only use money has to them is to buy weapons to do more killing. These murderous animals want pass up an opportunity to kill no more than a crackhead would pass up a rock of cocaine for the Lord's Supper. In all fairness, it did take the mullahs more than a thousand years to reach their 240 million murder milestone. It only took communist less than 80 years to reach their 100 million murder mark.

Who-U-Wid:

Is it any wonder Obama belongs to both camps? Don't be fooled by Obama's cut hair, nice suits and calm demeanor. There's a callous, cold blooded murderer beneath it all. Don't let the sheep's clothing fool you. Obama has proposed and fought for legislation that would allow partial birth abortion up until the moment of delivery. Legislation so wroth with the murder of innocent blood not even pro-baby killer senator Hillary Clinton, could support it. As an Illinois state senator the only time he showed up for work was to propose and enact such heinous legislation. Sometimes he was the only politician in Illinois voting in the affirmative. In most sane people's observations these traits are of a cold blooded murderer. There's blood thirst here. We only see the tip of the iceberg that's above the water mark. What's below is much bigger and much more dangerous. Behind this smoke is a raging fire.

What certifies Alinsky and his disciples as demonically charged is they see all of this carnage and waste of human life as a result of communism. Marx only had his vapid imagination to glean from. Still, Barak Obama, Bill and Hillary Clinton try to convince us it's good for us. They don't label communism as such, but couch it as from each according to his "ability" to each according to his "need." Again, communism is the lazy man's religion. Socialist in and out of pulpits has tied this suicide pact to the Bible, specific to Acts 2:45. The new church saints under the power and influence of the Holy Spirit, were selling possessions and goods and parting them to every man as he had need.   These people had all things in common.   They looked out for each other.   Not because heavy handed government official made them.   They were led by the Holy Spirit to do what's right.   The Holy Spirit does the same today.   It is done out of love and compassion for fellowman and not through some government go between with access to someone's pocket.

Just like Peter, James and John were Jesus' main disciples, they eventually reached prominence in the Christian world, so did Alinsky's main three disciples: Barak, Bill and Hillary have reached enormous prominence in the secular world.   While Peter, James and John went out preaching the good news of Jesus Christ.   Barak, Bill and Hillary have went about force-feeding us the bad news of communism.   The three of them might as well be some version of the Four Horsemen, plotting to rage their apocalypse on us all.   Death, disease, pestilence, and war will be our prophecy if these are left unchecked.   These imps are our adversaries. Who knows where all of this hate springs from?   Bad parents, college professors, environment, lack of moral clarity? What portal did the devil enter in to put these giant mad man chips on their shoulder? What we know is its present in all three.   Hate is a prerequisite to becoming a good Democrat.

Alinsky's "Rules for Radicals," which all three have followed to the letter to achieve their prominence, lesson one is to lie, lie, lie.   Who knows what shallow graves these know about?   The next is to agitate and keep agitating.   The next is to use words and phrases like "economic justice", "peace" and "democratic equally".   It sounds good to socially conscious ears, but they are nothing more than vices to lure in the great unwashed or low-information voter (these that hadn't spied out the lies and tricks of liberals).   Whose against peace, economic justice, and democratic equality?   These are no more than propagandist ruses, in the hands of Alinsky-ites. Through repeated agitation they get around to convincing you that the only way these ideals are possible is to rid ourselves of this system of free enterprise and capitalism in exchange for serfdom and communism.   They lie, lie, lie.   Subterfuge is a constant with them. Explain to me, how does destroying peoples livelihood, i.e. capitalism translate into all of this harmony and good vibrations?   That's why psych-ops is so important to these frauds. A great washed person will spot this idiocy a mile away.   But, the great unwashed, overtime, could be convinced that the destruction of the "means of production" will in affect produce an "abundance of goods". What the Alinskyites, try and tell us, is the best way to fix an oil leak on an airplane, is to load it with people and crash it into the side of a mountain.

Sure, they say there will be some pain and bugs to work out as you switch from HDTV back to the radio, from a Porche all the way back to a horse drawn buggy; from a jet plane to walking; from an ice box full of food to bare cupboards; from a nice comfortable warm house in the winter and a cool one in the summer, to you and your family living in an abandon car.   This has already taken place in a lot of quarters of America because of Obama's marxist bliss on the economy. Karl Marx, pretty much admitted this would be the case in his "lower phrase" of communism.   Some might refer to it as socialism.   But, it wouldn't be until you've gotten rid of all vestiges of the bourgeois and its class structure "and society inscribe on its banner: "from each according to his ability to each according to his need."   This is when "higher communism" kicks in.   The problem with this idiocy is, I was supplying my family's and my "needs" until you communist came in and shut down the factory I was working at.   I had a nice car, nice house, money in the bank, kids in school, good retirement and insurance plan and two weeks a year vacation along with sick leave.   I even had most weekends off.   Now that my family and I are now living on the streets, in plenty of "need" you tell me to wait on the guy with the "ability" to show up.   Well, didn't you shut down his factory too?   He is every bit as impoverished as I am.   Because in your rush to accomplish this imaginary Tibetan Buddhist Zen overtoned with the harmonic convergence myth, laced in the Age of Aquarius, nestled on some feng shui vibe in which we all just get alone, nobody has "ability" and every body's got "need".   Where is the "peace", "justice" and "democratic equality" in that?

Saul Alinsky, mimicked Karl Marx, in this way: "a marxist begins with the prime truth that all evils are caused by the exploitation of the proleriat by capitalist.   From this logic proceeds to the revolution to end capitalism, then into the third stage of reorganization into a new social order of the dictatorship of the proleriat, and finally the last stage– political paradise of communism" Alinsky admits that the workers will be dictated to by the communist leaders, once his means to make a living are taken away in this so-called "third stage".   But, in the "final stage" this "political paradise of communism" emerges.   What does that mean paradise for who?   Certainly not for the proletariat or working man and woman.   They have no means of support.   They are now homeless and starving. The central committee members are drowning in the finest champagne and choking on the best foods.   Again, where's the "peace", "justice" and "democratic equality" in that?

The Obamas and Clintons of the world want us to abandon all common sense notions and follow their lead of class envy and get evenwiththemism by hating the rich, which is anybody with one dollar more than you.   So we end up hating ourselves and everyone else, but them.   Then, for all of this hate, they offer nothing but misery.   A quick check on reality will reveal that these "dreadful" capitalist risk money to start businesses that employ us, while not their primary tend, it still bodes well for us.   While in their employ, we afford ourselves the "ability" to supply our own "needs" and not wait on some government entity or sovereign to provide it. In almost all incidences the employee gets paid before the employer.   He or she must first satisfy or reconcile the cost of goods sold margins, in which labor is almost always the highest number on the ledger.   If a profit is realized that pay period or quarter, it is put back into the business to expand or just stay afloat.   Sadly, most times it doesn't stay afloat.   It fails.   It's hard enough without a marxist like Obama doing everything he can to make them go under.   In too many cases Mr. and Mrs. Mom and Pop are living hand to mouth. And it may be years before they can catch their breath or take a day off.   Meanwhile, the proleriat is at home relaxed and enjoying their family, oblivious to what the capitalist or entrepreneur is faced with.   They don't have a money tree growing out back.   They ain't flush with cash, as an employee you might be living better than them. They get turned down for bank loans, just like the rest of us.   They are not winners of "life's lottery".   They are simply hard working Americans following a dream. Trying to make ends meet and payroll is an on edge occupation for small business people.   When the proleriat clocks out his work day ends. Not for the entrepreneur.   There is no time clock that sets the business owner free until the next day.   He or she packs it in their car and takes it home with them, if they have the luxury of even going home.   These people deserve our love, and our respect, not our wrath.   The Bible commands it.   People like Obama and the other Alinsky-ites should never be allowed to convince us otherwise. There are the job and opportunity producers, capitalist and the entrepreneurs. Then there are the job and opportunity killers, the communist in the Democratic Party. In the words of the late Bernie Mack: "Who-U-Wid?"

ABORTION

Again, the Democrats want to enslave us all. Nothing less than Stalinist styled control over our lives will suffice. At this point, they have already mentally prepared themselves to kill, murder, and assassinate, as many of us as needy to consolidate their power. Stalin, Hitler, and Mao Zedong, spared no human expense in achieving their totalitarian rule. By overseeing the senseless murder of some 55 million plus un-born babies in the United States since the Roe vs Wade decision, they have not only prepared themselves for the murdering rampage they plan, so has many in this nation been desensitized to the killing. Exponentially, these dead babies are twice the size of the populations of Canada and Australia combined. May God have mercy on our souls.

Democrats have seen so much bloodshed, they strain from breaking a yawn when you ask them about it. Know this, these murdered babies blood cry out to God from the ground and whatever garbage can out back, or cosmetic product their lifeless body's end up in. To the tune of 1.4 million abortions a year since Roe vs Wade, Democrats have fervently defended "a woman's right to choose." They have made sure through whatever legislative or court battles necessary that abortions remained "safe and legal" for any silly promiscuous female that wants one. Hell!" have more than one, some 45% of abortioners do. Democrats default or cliché retort is: "the women has the right to choose." Why didn't she choose not to have sex? Why didn't she choose contraception, or not try and trap the married man she was screwing around with? There are a number of choices to be made prior to this one. Even after conception there's still adoption or raising the child. Then again, those choices would cut away the $800-$2,500 per baby kill Democrat campaign donor Plan Parenthood, would get.

Democrats and their media buddies have pounded it into all of our heads that no one has the right to tell these naive twits what to do with their bodies. Yet, they and their marxist media buddies ad-nauseum tell the rest of us, we can't smoke or eat trans-saturated fats. Obamacare, says what we can and cannot do with our own bodies. I ask any sane person, which is more immediate and deadly, a puff on a cigarette, a piece of chicken, or the ripping away of the arms and legs of an unborn baby in an effort to kill it for the sole purpose of convenience. Anyone who wants to be governed by these sub-humans are every bit as sick, insane, and demonic as they are. These operate on a dis-socialtive plane that there is no God.   Therefore, there's no final arbiter or consequences for their actions.   Their thoughts are given over to a reprobate irrationalism.   So they are not conscious of a spiritual phenomenon call "sowing and reaping."   Since they don't retain God in their knowledge there is no right or wrong, only what they decide it to be from day to day.   Their situation is they're ethic. Whatever un-holy entity that they obey or worship demands the blood of innocent babies as their propitiation or sacrifice.   Eating the right food is also part of their godless religion.

OBAMA SCARE(Y):

The abortionist i.e., Democrats and Plan Parenthood, simply put, are eugenist hiding behind an elitist label.   They don't mind being called elitist because it hides their esoteric initiate.   They know something the rest of us "lesser" don't know or won't recognize, and that's abortion is more about streamlining the herd more than for "convenience" and money.   Sure, Plan Parenthood death mills, the "nonprofits" make billions of dollars but, that's just the bonus round of the killing game business.   More to the point, their founder Margaret Sanger (1879-1966), was more interested in the sterilization of "unfit (s)" as a means to eradicate them overtime.   While Sanger was anti-abortion because it is a danger to the health of the mother, she believed that sterilization and birth control were safer ways of accomplishing this goal.   Just like todays, elistist Sanger was a eugenist.   They believe if you're not of a Nordic race of "supermen" or stock, then you're better off dead or not coming into existence at all.   You had to be "well born" to satisfy her criteria for suitability.   The only humans that made the grade were wealthy White Anglo-Saxon Protestants (WASP) pure breds.   According to Sanger and other eugenist these had a superior genetic makeup.   If your DNA make-up didn't meet these standards, you weren't deserving of life.

American gynecologist William Goodell, advocated "castrating" and "spaying" the insane in 1882.   In 1883, Englishman and anthropologist Francis Galton, dubbed this selective breeding process "eugenics."   The American Breeder's Association", was the first eugenics body in the U.S.   This was 1906 and Alexander Graham Bell was a member.   By 1907, the State of Indiana passed the first eugenics-based compulsory sterilization law in the world. More than 3400 women were sterilized.   Thirty more states soon followed suit. The Indiana State Supreme Court, overturned the practice in 1921.   But, in 1927 the U.S. Supreme Court ruled (Buck vs Bell) that the state of Virginia could sterilize anybody it deemed "unfit." By the 1930's, forced sterilizations were between 2,000-4,000 a year in the United States.   Early on, the eugenics movement was supported financially by The Harriman railroad fortune; the Rockefeller Foundation; and the Carnegie Institution – which recommended "euthanasia" as a solution to cleanse society of its "unfits."

Sanger called immigrants "feeble minded" "idiots," "morons" "insane," "suphillic," "epileptic," "criminal" "prostitute" "paupers" and "fiends."   The Corning, New York native and former nurse didn't think much of Southern Whites either.   She called them, "shiftless," "ignorant" and a "worthless class of anti-social" people.   She wasn't that complementary of Blacks.   She called us a "mass of ignorant

Negroes still breeding carelessly and disastrously." So that the increase amongst Blacks, even more than the increase among Whites, is from that part of the population least intelligent and fit and least able to rear their children properly. The Klu Klux Klan itinerant speaker didn't stop there. She wrote that Blacks were "genetically inferior" spawning human weeds," "reckless breeders" who never should have been born."

Despite all of this indignation toward Black people, Black elites praised and applauded her work in "birth control" "women health issues" and "family planning." Amongst her Black intellectual admirers were WEB Dubois, William Clayton Powell, and Dr. Martin Luther King Jr., who received the first Margaret Sanger award given by Plan Parenthood in 1966.

Sanger and colleague Dr. Harry Laughlin believed that sterilizing "unfits" like Black people would be the "salvation of American civilization." If this woman was alive today she would have either Democrat minority leader of the House Nancy Pelosis's job, or senate Democrat leader Harry Reid's. Certainly, she would be Barak Obamas, top adviser. Not just on the eradication of Black folk but, on foreign policy and on the economy. She couldn't do worse than the incompetent children working for him now. Obama would be so impress with her utter disdain for people, that he would put her chariot right behind his, pull off his signet ring give it to her, and sport her with designer clothes and gold bling. Democrats and Time magazine would name her person of the millennium. No doubt, she would be the DNC's convention's keynote speaker. She would have an open invitation to speak at all of the NAACP gatherings. These barbarians would carry her around on their shoulders and chant "Ding Dong the wicked witch is alive and well" – and "Oh we love the old one." Even though she died in 1966 at the age of 86, the Democrat party, with the civil rights cabal as their accomplices, has continued her dream of exterminating the Black race. Never in history has there been a more useless and ass backwards cadre of human debris as the civil rights movement members'. Sanger herself, was against abortion but, once the Supreme Court decided Roe vs Wade, her baby, Plan Parenthood, started aborting Black babies. Almost simultaneously, Democrats put "Title X" on Richard Nixon's desk which put the United State's government in the baby killing business by paying for abortions for poor women. Republican presidents since have fought to either eliminate the bill, or drastically decrease its funding. Of course, Democrat presidents have done just the opposite. Democrats and the marxist media hide the wholesale slaughter of human beings behind the titles of "preventive health services" and "family planning." With more than one Black baby being aborted for every two non-Black babies and Black people being roughly 13% of the population, they can live with that collateral damage, trade off and attrition rate.

Note: Perhaps, one of the most egregious episodes in the whole atrocious abortion and baby killing sager, happened back in 1982. There were 17,000 fetuses discovered at the home of Malvin Weisberg, in Woodland Hills, California, a Los Angeles suburb. Weisberg, was the owner of Medical Analytical Laboratories located in Santa Monica. His company was contracted to dispose of the fetuses in a "humane" way.   At least 16,000 of these precious babies, were found in a dumpster or container he rented from Martin Container Company, who made the discovery after repossessing it after receiving a bad check from Weisberg. Sad and sickening as this was, the feminist movement along with the ACLU and a godless judge, moved in to deny the 17,000 fetuses a proper or Christian burial.   Then President Ronald Reagan, calling it a "national tragedy" (Barak Obama, would call it and abortion a "national treasure"), wrote a letter urging a memorial service for the babies. But, the feminazi movement and ACLU sued, and Los Angeles, Superior Court Judge, Eli Chernow, agreed that the service or ceremony would violate "the separation of church and state."   This demented bastard went on to say "fetal remains are normally incinerated without ceremony.   The intended burial ceremony will enlist the prestige and power of the state"…The Catholic League (one of the pro-life groups offering a honorable burial at their own expense) is a religious organization which regards the fetuses as human (what else were they elephant, cat or dog remains) and abortion as murder" (what else do you call it when an innocent human life is snuffed out by the hands of another) we perceived that the intended burial ceremony will be strictly strunized and must be invalid."   What?   Did someone call for a court appointed priest, rabbi or preacher to do the last rites?   Was someone asking for government paid gravediggers?   Was someone demanding they be buried at a city, state or national park?   No, then where was the governments liability, injure, or "prestige."   Just like Joseph of Arimathea, asked for the body of Jesus Christ, and buried Him in his own grave tomb at his own expense so

did these anti-murder pro-life saints ask for the bodies of these 17,000 babies to bury at their own expense.   The "power of the state" had no issue here.   Unless you argue that the state owned the fetuses because it paid for the abortions and through extension and purchase they owned them.   Someone pointed out that at least 70% of the fetuses were Black babies, and it's known that upwards of 80% of Plan Parenthood murder mills are located in the Black community; we can then extrapolate that "Title X" money was used to commit these murders, with the mother's full advice and consent provoked.   With this preponderance, the government makes it "separation of church and state" half ass argument.   Valhalla Memorial cemetery, offered to bury the 193 fetuses that was aborted beyond, then California's 20 week gestation period cut off.   Judge Chernow, in his ruling overturned it, calling it "unconstitutional."   Roe vs Wade allowed for 23 weeks. We're way pass that now on our slippery slope of moral depravity.   Both Barak Obama, and Bill Clinton, advocates "a day of birth" partial birth abortion bill.   The thrust was this" the feminazis, the ACLU and a liberal judge wanted to remove or blot out the very notion that these fetuses were of human origin.   Therefore skirting their "due process" rights, and not evoking their habeas corpus.   These have prospered on two concepts of demonic delusion long enough, and that's aborted fetuses are nothing more than globs of flesh or tissue.   The other, is anything they want to start or stop in our society, especially that of a religious nature, they simply apply the "separation of church and state" app and magically it's done.   There are enough lawless, godless, and gutless judges up and down the

Appellate and Supreme Court chain, Democrats have made sure of it, that will rule in their favor, despite what congress or establish law says.   These renegades love legislating from the bench anyway.   Their Stalinist inclinations provokes them. They are not constrained by conscience nor constitutional laws.   They were wiping their asses with the Constitution long before Obama came along and started wiping his.   The "establishment clause" or "wall of separation" between "church and state"," originally coined by Thomas Jefferson, simply put, meant that the state could not establish a religion, nor favor one over another. Neither could it prohibit the free exercise of religion, short of a "compelling interest" i.e., satan worship and human sacrifices.   This was the case up until Engel V. Vitale (1964) and Abington V. Schempp (1963).   Then this, takes us back to abortion, and the Declaration of Independents, and its" life liberty and pursuit of happiness" preamble and unalienable rights mention which the government is duly sworn to protect has to be revisited.   Under the most bizarre interpretation of the "wall of separation" statute, could there be a finding that church cannot involve itself in the affairs of government.   If so, you eliminate much of the 15th Amendment.   Then Christians, Jews, and Moslems wouldn't be allowed to vote, because of their religious affiliations.   Neither would they be allowed to serve in any government capacity.   Trust me, the Obama regime via Attorney General Eric Holder, and the Democrat party are feverishly working on applying the separation of church and state (as they interpret it) clause to Evangelicals. Someone mention through Sharia law.   Judges in Michigan are already using it to decide cases.   Taking their

*cue from people like Oliver Wendell Holmes, (1841-1932)
and Woodrow Wilson (1856-1924), liberals love to refer to
the Constitution as a "living document." Calling
themselves pragmatist, they fear monger and lie, saying the
Constitution, written by White men, supported slavery.
But, it was changing morals and attitudes that stopped it.
No, it was White Democrats that supported it. With White
and Black Republicans, using things like the Emancipation
Proclamation, the 13th, 14th, and 15th Amendments, and
Reconstruction, all spoils of their Civil War victory to stop it.
By calling the Constitution a "living document, they can
bend, mold, shape, and change it into anything they want it
to be or mean; which always result in a loss of freedoms for
the rest of us.*

A PRELUDE TO A KILL:

*Note: Revisiting the issue of abortion, the Supreme Court
then (1973), decided Roe vs Wade on the 14th amendment's
"due process" clause along with some confluence of a
"right to privacy" clause not found in the 14th Amendment
to make the long jumper's leap to reach its fraudulent
decision. In their jump, they leapt over the Constitution's
preamble of…" to establish justice, insure domestic
tranquility, provide for the common defense, promote the
general welfare"…, The Warren Court, gave the unborn no
assurance of "tranquility", no "defense", their "welfare"
certainly was not considered, and they receive no justice
from the courts bogus ruling. In bastardizing the "due
process" clause it invoked or found a "right to privacy."*

Something the rest of us couldn't see or find using Berkeley's TEAM microscope.   The court conjured it from whole cloth and thin air as if it were a magic act. A magic act has more to work with.   This is how a "living" constitution works.   The 14th amendment was another outgrowth of Abe Lincoln, and the Republican Party's efforts to protect freed slaves from the Democrat party. It's "due process" clause is this: a government has to give due process before it can take away a person's life liberty or property.   In short, there has to be a trial, where evidence is presented by the state to prove its case against a person or company.   But, in its convolution, the Supreme Court, used it to deny the unborn child due process.   Using the original intent of the statue, before the life of the unborn is taken, and its liberties infringed or injured, it has to be given a trial.   Outside of the mother's life, what evidence or charges can the state or the mother bring that would warrant the death penalty.   By far, they are the most innocent among us.   This is why they don't allow us, even with our own imaginations, to see the color of their eyes and hair.   Things like their life's potential and contributions to mankind might have been, are very much off limits.   How many Albert Schwetzers, Mother Theresas, Martin Luther King Jrs, Hank Aaron's, Albert Einsteins, and yes, Barak Obamas have died at the hands of a Mengelian abortionist. The feminist fight so hard and pollute the lexicon with phrases like "only a glob of tissue" They and their marxist media friends deny the fetus human status at every turn.

We have murderers sentenced to life in prison, but released after serving a few years.   The ones that rarely get the death penalty, may sit on death row for up to 25 years, before being executed.   The same liberal mind that beats-off at a women executing her child without any due process, do everything imaginable to save these scumbags from receiving their due, even after an endless number of due process trials.

In terms of the pretzeled logic of "right of privacy" in the Roe vs Wade case, you can hide AIDS and many other medical conditions, but, you can't hide a pregnancy.   In a few months people will be telling her she's not only putting on weight, but why.   Secrecy and privacy, the same as AIDS, may have been the cause but at some point, this thing climbs a roof top and shouts.   It doesn't go unnoticed by the passerby.   By nature and course she has no privacy. Victoria's, Betty or Luann's secret is out.   Maybe you invoke a right to privacy for the AIDS carrier, but not the women with the extra-large stomach.   If so, you give her an extra-large burka not a license to kill her unborn child. Or, we dig further down the hole of human depravity and say her privacy is more important than her child's life.

I would love to see a Faye Wattleston, argue privacy as a prelude to killing while standing next to an axe murderer, complete with Jason mask and sharp object.   No, she would find religion real quick and preach: "Thou shalt not kill." By using the Supreme Court, and Wattleston's logic, the axe murderer's privacy rights are infringed if he is not allowed to have a whack or two at her neck.   Here, the slippery slope gets up to speed.   Other than the 10th Amendment (1791), which put abortion under the individual state's province, this is why legal scholars refer to Roe vs Wade as bad law.   It hangs on the flimsiest thread of human reasoning.   Where does this right of privacy, (nee, right to

kill) ends?   Murder rates in America have soared since Roe
vs Wade.   Once you announce something is legal, then it
becomes okay to do.   People drive, hunt, fish, teach,
marry…etc, once the government hands them a license.
The license is a prelude to the action; why should killing be
any different?   Frankly, it's all worn a little too thin with
me.   What about you?

True to form, the New York Urban League, invited the
weasel into the chicken coup.   In 1929 they asked Sanger, to
open a clinic in Harlem.   Ms. Sanger, with the Great
Depression at full roar, pawned her wares of family planning,
women health, and every child should be born into a
financially and mentally stabled home off on Black preachers.
They then passed the Jonestown elixir out to their
congregates.   Using this criterium, I dare say 90% of Black
folk then, and quite a few now, would have never been born.
This demon had the uncanny ability to speak in front of Black
congregations and at Klu Klux Klan rallies with the ease of
water flowing down stream.   Her svengalli charm, convinced
both opposite ends of the political spectrum that she had their
best interest at heart.   She told Black elites she wanted to
keep their population growth down.   She told the Democrat
party's Klu Klux Klan auxillary she wanted to elimate the
Black race.   It was win win for her.   Bill Clinton could speak
to both groups at the same time in the same hall, with them
sitting next to each other, and convince both groups that he
understood their issues and had plans to resolve them.   Both
would leave the campaign rally convinced, Bill was their man.
For years, that's what he did as Arkansas governor.

Sanger, was never openly hostile or racist. Face to face, she treated Black people with the utmost of respect and demanded her employees did the same. She taught the Democrat party well. She put Black intellectuals like WEB Dubois, on her board committees and Black doctors in her "Negro Project" clinics. Upwards of 80% of her "Negro Project" clinics now known as Plan Parenthood, still, with the blessings of the civil rights conspiracy are in inner city communities. Plan Parenthood has one hundred of these "Negro project" clinics in predominately Black schools around the country. One parent called this "ugly apartheid." The estimates since 1973 (Roe vs Wade) are that between 13 and 26 million Black babies were killed in abortion murder mills. Black women represent less than 8% of the overall population. Yet, conservatively speaking, they have accounted for more than 35% of these abortions. Only White liberals and the worthless civil rights conspiracy can pat themselves on the back at this atrocity. Plan Parenthood's business is killing and business is good. Especially, when it comes to Black babies.

This is why I warn the Hispanic community not to allow the Democrat party and the marxist news media pick its leaders. My heart felt advice is to speak individually by voting individually. But, first you must think for yourself. Group think is dangerous because it's subjective and not objective. People are then licensed to control and play with your emotions. Especially when the person chosen as your representative is speaking only for the Democrat party and their own self-interest and not what's best for you.

Since the turn of the 19th century the civil rights scum has been speaking for Black people. Look where it's gotten us.   Upward of 26 million Black babies killed. Not to mention the sterilization of Black women, fatherless generations of Black children, thrown away children; we're more than half the U.S. prison population, high-school dropout rates, hopelessness, despair, crumbling schools, and high unemployment rates. In addition to all of this, permanent status at the very bottom of the economic totem pole.   My warning to the Hispanic community is don't lose your family unit, your hard work ethic, and your rich cultural future by getting into bed with the Democrats.   If you do, you will be the ones being sodomized, and Democrats are not known for using lubricants.

Afterwards, Ms. Myra asked Rusty, "well aren't you going to thank me…? " Democrats will demand gratitude for them screwing you over.   Look at how they have screwed Blacks over for all of these many years.   Still, with the hutspah of God Almighty, they demand we Black folks stay one hundred and ten percent loyal to them.   Democrats want to make Hispanic wards of the state.   If someone like myself ("a nigger that dares to think for himself") step out of line, I am called a "sell out" or "Uncle Tom."   Remember what they did to Clarence Thomas.   I am not under no circumstances allowed to vote for, or support any candidate I might choose to.   I can only vote for who the party tells me to vote for. We have our own little communist island working here. Democrats can't get over the fact that we are no longer their slaves and personal chattel, nether can a lot of Black folk.   If your White, Jewish or Hispanic your allowed some leeway. For us former Democrat party chattelites, no such liberty is allotted.   There are plenty of plantation dwelling "house nigger" ready to put me back on the road to serfdom if I

swerve to the right.   There is no sane reason to vote for a
Democrat.   Nothing good will ever come of it.   Any
perceived good, is only a marxist media fabrication and if they
don't care about the most innocent among us, then how can
you argue they care for you?   All they care about is your vote.
No lie or promise is too big or ridiculous to tell you, to get it.

Tonya L. Green (Concerned Women of America), says
that the reasons for Black elites falling for the Negro Project's
smoke and mirror is "they see birth control as a way of
attaining economic empowerment, elevate the race, and
garner the respect of Whites".   No doubt Ms. Green, is on
point with her assessments.   So I ask these dupes both dead
and alive, how do you elevate your race by wiping it out?   As
for "empowerment," the more the merrier.   In terms of
impressing White people,   we should have no other gods
before Him.   We have made the Democrats our god in our
quest for race elevation and empowerment. Organizations like
"LEARN" (Life, Education, and Research Network) (mahal.
Abortionfact.com – learn) (please donate), a Black pastors
group dedicated to stopping the genocide of Black babies by
putting an end to abortion, are laugh at and scorned by other
Black preachers who have bowed their knee for years now to
Democrats.   It always amazes me what Black preachers want
preach about for fear of offending some Democrat.   Too
often, Black folk ridicule and make fun of those in the
community attempting to bring positive change.   At the same
time, hi-fiving drug dealers, gangster rappers, and race
hustlers.   There's a whole lot of mirror time and
self-examination needed for our survivor.   Attorney General
Eric Holder, said he wanted to have a "conversation about
race" in this country.   "Let's have it!" But, you want do all

the talking.   Now let's see if these "cowards" show up.

Obama, oblivious to the world outside of his head and its morals and how it really works, sticks his fingers once again in the eyes of every decent American.   Being the first president to do so, he attends a Plan Parenthood conference and makes a speech. He seemed gitty beyond control.   He could hardly control the Jihadist blood thirsty streak going down his back.   It was like all the cares in the world (not that he has any) melted away.   It is Calgon "take me away" for him when he bathe in the agilation of his likeminded fellow feminazis.   His mecca nirvana goes off the charts.   I dare anyone to produce a picture of Obama with a bigger smile on his face.   His speech was filled with the same old liberal platitudes that are tired and worn out to thinking people.   The crazy scary guy spoke about the lives of women "saved" by Plan Parenthood, and how they have "empowered" woman. Scary guy, actually credited PPH with helping women with "fertility" and curing them of cancer.   First of all, I doubt if Plan Parenthood has saved any women's life.   Still, if they have, let's compare that to the millions upon millions of lives they have assisted in taking.   As far as "fertility" problems, concerned if you define the direct or indirect sterilization of women as helping, then yes.   In terms of "empowering women", once a women aborts her baby she loses all power over the father.   Her control over his life money and whereabouts for the next 18 to 19 years is gone. Moreover, what kind of power is there without a child loving you back? The hand that rocks the cradle and all that.   It ain't a lot of ball players shouting "hi dad."   Trust me, the last thing a women feels is "empowered" after allowing the abortionist to kill her child.   In almost all cases that's a regret she carries

with her for the rest of her life.   Where's the power in that?
Even those who shrug it off as if it's no big deal, in their alone
time it's there.   The memory of the massacre and lost is still
there.   What color would the hair and eyes might have been,
it's there.   No women's right "empowerment" crap will erase
it.   The blood is on her hands.   It's on the abortionist hands
and everybody's hands who ever voted for a pro-choice
politicians who voted for the public funding of Sanger's
Negro project "clinics. That being said, only the Blood of
Jesus can wash the blood, the pain, the lost, and depression
away.   He wants to turn their mess into a miracle. Just like He
did for Norma McCorvey.   She was the Jane Roe, in Roe vs
Wade.   The child she wanted to abort she carried to term and
gave up for adoption.   Now she's a spokesperson for
abolishing abortion.   The murdered baby's blood is on the
hands of Barak Obama, but he likes seeing it there.
Especially doing he and his wife's pentagram and cauldron
worship services.   It cuts out the need for the fresh born baby,
dagger and alter portion of their worship service.   One
wonders when the sum total of Women's Lib or Rights is
killing babies.   Sometimes in their religion you can substitute
goat's blood for humans.   These imps prefer humans.

Plan Parenthood curing cancer, was the most ridicules
statement Obama has ever uttered in his life.   Lord knows,
most have been off the wall crazy. But this one takes the cake,
bakes the cake, and eats the cake.   Somehow I don't see a
woman suffering with cancer turning to Plan Parenthood for a
cure.   If they got people believing this BS (Barbara
Streisand) then I say no matter what they pay their public
relations and lobbyist people, it's not enough.   The
quarterback with the broken leg don't go to the 300+ pound

defensive lineman who broke it to fix it.   In short, abortions cause cancer.   I discuss this in my upcoming book so I want give it depth here.   The research proves it.   The American Cancer Society was browbeaten, threatened and bribed into changing their research model to curtail its results by Democrats in congress.   The pro-baby killing lobby has done everything within its considerable power to squash any statements or public debate concerning it.   So has the marxist media.   Again, killing is their business, and they want to keep business good.   I remember Oprah Winfrey, got so indignant with the doctor who first made the link between abortion and breast cancer, she threw him off her show.   My guess was she had once had a Plan Parenthood business card in her purse.   For a friend, of course.   Another guess of mine, is that was the reason the Susan G. Komen Foundation wanted to cut ties with PPH.   Remember how crazy those bastards went over that one.   Even Matt Lauer, was beside himself.   They tell us skin cancer is the number one cancer women get but, we're not buying that Barbara Streisand.   We know its breast cancer.   And the number one, two, and three cause of breast cancer is abortion.   The abortionist either want tell a women this or can't.   Someone seeking one should know their chances of getting breast cancer greatly increases. So how crazy is it, that a woman might seek cancer relief from the monsters that caused it.   Then again, getting paid on the front end for causing the cancer, and then again on the backend for attempting to cure it, is one hellified business model.

    If the National Football League want be embarrassed for itself, then I will for them.   For four weeks out of the season these dupes parade around in pink costumes.   The last thing most women want to see is a man who is suppose to represent the most macho profession known to man running around in what appears to be tutus.   I mean, have I just tuned into a NFL game or a production of Swan Lake.   Given that NFL players can't touch each other no more, they can only pirouette and bow, Swan Lake is a safe bet.   They remind you of drag queens and pimped-out flamingos.   All that's missing are the boas and Max-Factor.   With political correctness taking over the sport, let's give that a little time.   The "throwback" uniforms are sometimes horrific but, the leotards and tights are more than most can take. The sad thing is the lobbyist who convinced the NFL to wear all of this pink is laughing themselves silly at what they have accomplished; making grown burly men dress up in ballet outfits.   They can't believe the utter fools and mockery they are making of America's greatest pastime. Political correctos love mocking anything American.   This would be silly even if it were golf or tennis. Let them try this crap with the Wimbledon committee and see what a lashing they will get.   What's even more sadder and heartbreaking is the players think they are doing something to bring awareness to breast cancer and find a cure.   The only thing they are doing is hurting viewership. If they really want to bring awareness and a cure to breast cancer, put a picture of an aborted fetus on the side of their helmets.   That should do it.

SLIP SLIDING AWAY:

If Obamacare is allowed to go to fruition, abortion will be the only medical procedure doctors will be allowed or force to perform.   There will be no money for anything else, unless you're part of the elites, or ruling class.   Margaret

Sanger, and the Democrat party has had their "Negro Project to rid the planet of Black people and other "unfits." So did Adolf Hitler, and the Nazi party had their "final solution", to rid the planet of Jews and other "unfits" Obama's front man on eugenics is Kathleen Sebilus, Hitler's was Ernst Rudin, who told an American audience that the Third Reich adopted it's sterilization plan from Californian's forced sterilization law. The author of the law Paul Popenoe, before reinventing himself into a marriage counselor, and Mr. Family values after World War II, estimated that some 5 to 10 million Americans might qualify for forced sterilization. California, out force sterilized the other states combined. They are still, to this day, illegally forcing female prisoners into having tubal ligations.

Rudin, and the Nazis were late to the force sterilization nightmare. We got started in 1906 with the state of Indiana forcing its "unfits" (mental defectives, Black women, poor White women, criminals) to undergo sterilization. Before long, other states had passed similar legislation. The slippery slope had begun. It wasn't until the early 1930's after reading Popenoe's and Sanger's writings on the subject that the Nazis became interested and worked feverishly to get laws pass. The propagandist method they use, was tried and true: "healthcare savings". They used posters of adults with some kind of mental or physical defect in a wheelchair with the caption saying the amount of money… no, that's how they got the euthanasia laws enacted. Once they got eugenics passed using the threat of the Aryan or Nordic race being contaminated with the blood or genes of the "unfit" then the slippery slope and race to utter depravity was on. Once the German people allowed themselves to be manipulated into racial purity as a man-made necessity, then from the forced sterilization of upwards of 400,000 people to saving money on healthcare cost by euthanizing 275,000, to the systematic murder of 6 million people, mostly Jews, as an answer to the question of the citizenship or proper treatment of Jews that combinated into the Reichs "final solution". It didn't end there, when the tally of dead and displaced people was finalized – near 20 million people were killed and another 10 to 15 million were displaced. It all got started with the forced sterilization of the "unfits".

The Negro Project in America began with the sterilization of a few hundred people. Forced sterilization in Germany, begun with a few thousand "unfits" and ended up with more than 6 million Jews being murdered along with millions of others being killed or displaced. Since the Negro project got started in the late 1930's, 55 plus million babies have been murdered. Obamacare, reads like a Nazi handbook on forced sterilization and euthanasia. If allowed to continue, it would put us on a trajectory parallel to the crash and burn of Hitler's Third Reich. The Hindenburg's crash and burn will seem like a campfire compared to the slaughter that awaits us with Obamacare.

Obama and the Democrats sold his monstrosity on the healthcare saving lie. The same way the Nazis sold euthanasia. When Sara Palin, summed up the whole 2200 + pages of the small print legaleed diction (without reading a word of it), in two words, "death panels," the liberal establishment went crazy. You know what dog got hit by the rock you threw by which one howls. The Democrats and the marxist media, none of which read the bill or investigated her statement, did what they do best, circle the wagons and howl foul.   If Obamacare has a snowball chance in hell of working for a very short period, hundreds of thousands of people, mostly the elderly and "unfit" would have to be denied medical help or coverage.   Whether a person or panel, someone will have to decide who gets help and who doesn't.   Obama will be too busy playing golf, with Walter Reed, and a team of doctors at his disposal.   Obama himself, used "end of life usefulness," and "cost outweighing the benefits" language.   His rhetoric or sales-pitch wasn't that cryptic.   I didn't hear a lot of nuance concerning the rationing of healthcare services.   Hell!" he talked about denying his own grandmother, who raised him, healthcare coverage because of "end of life usefulness."   Because he has no natural affection, he was oblivious to how bad that made him look, not only as an ungrateful grandson, but as person.   His staff learned early on to keep a hearing device in his ear.   He's quick to go off strip and scare people by talking up the virtues of marxism, as if he were telling how to find Leprechaun's gold.   He's oblivious to how he panics people when he starts talking about what he really wants to do.   So they know to keep their finger on the mute button.

Most of what Obama wants to do is in the Obama scare healthcare debacle.   It's his vehicle for causing as much hurt, pain, suffering, death, and disease to the American people as possible.   In addition to stripping away every freedom we have ever known.   He hates America that much, all leftist do.   For all of her deviousness and extermination schemes Margaret Sanger, was a thousand times more humane than Obama and the Democrat party.   In fact, I'll say she was 55 plus million more times humane.   There is no more guessing at his Manchurian mission.   He is Raymond Shaw, and has seen the queen of diamonds. The communist that have mentored him all of his life can only be awed by his success and their brainwashing him. Bill Clinton, spent several months back in the 60's in cold war Russia as a Rhodes Scholar, and we still don't know what he did while there. We can guess.

According to Alex Jones, of Infowars.com Obama scare reads like a eugenics program. He says the bill "clearly advocates a eugenics-based rationing system." Language in the bill like, "citizens are not basic and should not be guaranteed," support his conclusion. A lot of the law reads like Hitler's, eugenist wrote it. Jones said that the law contains a "corps" clause. This so-called "corps" clause says "home health care visits to access the designated family's economic self-sufficiency, employment, school readiness, and educational achievement." All this seems necessary and altruistic but, it leans upon that slippery slope that the late Senator Daniel Moynihan, echoed by Rush Limbaugh and others concerning our moral decline. This is "boob bait for the bubbas." Notwithstanding, its none of the governments business what our financial status is. Once the tax check is in the mail, that's it. They neither have any business in sticking their nose into how we raise our children. Liberals have no problems with the government telling us what to do, except when it comes to abortion. There is a quest to define deviancy down, even further. Like most cancers, this one won't localize, just spread and kill. The idiots, or people who refuse to be responsible for their own lives, eat this kind of bait and switch, cradle to grave, Bataan death march and government meddling up. This is scary stuff. The idiots don't hear the march of jack booted thugs coming up from behind, marching in double time. If they did, they'd think they were bringing more government handouts.   May be more minutes for their Obama phones.   They walk around with this fool's gold like it were money in the bank. The jack booted army is all this "corp" is. It's Obama and the Democrats gestapo. They'll force their way into your home and assess if you are financially able to support your family.   With Obama's economy, chances are you want be. Then they'll take your children and whatever else they want away from you.   Just like Hitler, when he and the Nazis confiscated people's boys for his youth movement, Obama has enacted his "youth camp". Then with the "school readiness" and "educational achievement" license in pocket, if your children are not straight "A" students they will deem them retarded or mentally disabled, sterilized or euthanize them under the guise of healthcare savings and racial purity.   Just like the images you see in a horror film, this is not a movie nor a bad dream.   If only it were.   This is scary, scary stuff.   Once the government gets this camel's head under the tent, "IT'S OVER!"   The sleigh ride down the slippery slope will be complete.

Like the down loading green slides across it's bar on your computer screen before the downloading is complete, how far down are we now on the slippery slope with Obama and the Democrat's final solution, or Negro project for us all? Are we at 5%, 20% or 99%?   All this while most of the Republican party coward in fear of being called racist for really challenging Obama on this scary stuff.   They don't or won't get it.   The Democrats marxist media, and race hustlers, will call them racist no matter what they do or say. These castrated passives need to know we got a country to save. This should mean more to them than their political offices. It's time they untie their tubes and grow a pair. The Democrats, the marxist media and the race hustlers, they are the real racist as this book proves time and time again. The information is now available to them and the American people. "SO FIGHT!" with everything you've got. Stop being afraid and scared of these bastards. If you don't this country will, in the words of Paul Simon, "go slip sliding away".

LET'S ROLL:

It's obvious to anyone who would dare take notice, what the Democrats are prepared to do to the rest of us if they cannot only watch the senseless slaughter of the most innocent among us but, they do everything humanly possible to defend and protect it. Remember, Joseph Stalin, played nice or Robin Hood, with the peasants, and proleriats in Russia, promising to take from the rich and bourgeois to give to them. While waiting by the tracks for the gravy train to arrive, it came loaded with tanks and Red army soldiers. In his bait and switch tactic Stalin, rolled on the peasants, proleriat and the bourgeois. The rich had means to escape to America and other countries. The others smelved into Stalin's regime, becoming part of the privileged and ruling class. Much the same way the Spielberg, Katzenberger and Warren Buffets, have become buddy, buddy with the Obama regime. Once Steve Jobs figured out that lil Barry had no intentions of doing anything, other than taxing and regulating American business out of existence, he slunk away. The Spielbergs and Katzenbergers are naïve twits. Buffet, seeks his own gain and advantage.   Still, all three have private jets fueled loaded with cash (all they hadn't transferred to offshore accounts) ready to leave America at a moment's notice if little Barry Stalin, gets his way.   Jorge' warned a long time ago about forgetting the pass in exchange for reliving it.

Even with the 43 million Stalin has reportedly killed, it's still ten million less than that the Democrats and their adjuncts (Womans Libs, PPH, civil rights cabal, renegade judges) have aided in murdering.   That's 30 million more than the bubonic plague killed in Europe in the 14th century.   Once killing humans in the womb becomes acceptable the way killing Jews and other undesirables did in WW2's Germany, let us ask ourselves how far are we from making the leap to killing us outside of the womb?   The German people accepted killing Jews as a necessary evil, killing is killing.   Once the reprobate mind kicks in, killing outside of the womb is no more a moral dilemma.   There is no depth man's depravity knows.   There is only an awaiting abyss.   Once you give license for convience killing, you give that same license to all kinds.   In the body cancer rarely localize.   It spreads until it's stopped or cut out.   In too many cases, cancer wins.

Eddie B. warned us "all that is necessary for the triumph of evil is that good men do nothing."   Economist Milton Friedman, said that "The normal state of man is misery and tyranny Freedom is not a natural phenomenon."   Thomas Jefferson said the tree of liberty must be refresh from time to time with the blood of patriots and tyrants.   Big government types need to know, if you go pass this point we start shooting.   A point in my estimation America's tyrant class crossed a long time ago.   We must be of a mind to take the fight to them, before they become embolden to roll on us.   We can't wait for their total mobilization. They advance daily. What redress do we have?   The courts are no longer willing to protect us and elected officials seemingly are in retreat. We haven't given God any reason to have our backs so what arrows are left in our quiver?   What bullets remain?   Forget New Year's celebration keep the powder dry and the bullets near and dear.   We must adopt an "out of my cold dead hand" posture.   The barbarians are at the gate.

We can't rely on political cowards like Republican Senator John McCain, or any of the establishment Republicans.   They only serve at their masters, the marxist media pleasure.   They are afraid of their own political shadows.   More than anything the McCainiacs value the blessing of the New York Times, still the liberal media hates them.   At times, these broken clocks get it right.   But, we now stand at a precipus in time where half way Republicanism want get it done. You're either all the way for us, or all the way against us.   Luke warm is not an option. At this juncture, we need those brave "Radical Republicans," lead by Lincoln, Grant, and Sherman, who rolled into Southern states like Georgia, the Carolinas and others and gave their arms, legs and lives to end the tyranny of slavery: and they didn't negotiate some 3/5 of a man treaty or compromise like a McCain moderate would have done.   We need the original "Minute-men" of the American Revolution; those Tea Party Patriots that know that freedom is not a "natural phenomenon" but must be earned with "the blood of patriots and tyrants."   We call forth those men who knows that a little rebellion now and then is a good thing; and that the tree of liberty must be "refreshed". "Every freedom loving American that knows that misery and tyranny are the "natural state of man" must stand ready to enter the fray and not sit idly by and sing que sera sera.   All hands are needed on deck with guns loaded and cocked.   We have a country to save.   Evil has made its bid at triumph, what will good men do?

On the way to their final solution Obama and the Democrats have taken over healthcare, Wall Street, schools, parental notification, the tax code, and many parts of the Republican party.   Now they stand poised to take over us. With their forward and our retreat, how long before they suspend posse comatitus and declare marshall law and Obama declare himself premier leader and the ballot box invalid.   He has already declared the Constitution non invoid and himself dictator with a touch of deity.   With the homosexuals taking over the military, the deputizing of illegal aliens, Fast and Furious was nothing more than a dry run on the logistic of supplying the gringo's with guns to do the Alamo and Poncho Villa thing again.   Their strategy: if Texas falls so goes the country.

Obama is shutting down gun manufacturers, Iran can become a terrorist state with nuclear bombs.   China and Russia are rebuilding.   Obama is rooting for global annihilation of western civilization.   His hate doesn't stop at these shores.   This guy is serious about the dreams of his leftist father, deadly serious.   The survivalist don't seem so crazy and paranoid now.   Ruby Ridge and Waco didn't wake us up, will this?   Yes, we are up to speed now?

There will be a 100 Million Man March on Washington D.C.   The protest signs will only read the Holy Bible and Smith and Wesson.   Jesus said "But now."   It's time for him who ain't packing to go and pawn something and scrap on Luke 22:36 (NDV)   The chants will not be "we want our country back", BUT WE COME TO TAKE OUR COUNTRY BACK. And restore our Constitution and kick out the money changers.   The tyrants don't get to decide the outcome of the 100 Million Man March.   Resistance will be futile.   They seek their Red Dawn confrontation, let make them think twice.   We need all one hundred million to show up.   We all carry this cross together.   If we're one short then Obama, and his marxist media want take us serious.   They will then give all of the attention to the ten or so counter protesters that show up.   The Occupy Wall Street, street trash types.   Where there's 100 million men there's bound to be 300 million women and children.   All it took years for them to take from us, we take back in a day.   We have suffered your insolence long enough.   Now the violent take it all back by force.   To this cause, we offer our blood, toil, tears and sweat.   We will fight on the beaches, the landing grounds, the fields, in the streets, in the hills; we will never surrender. The revolution will not be televised so be there to see for yourselves.   Nothing we'll doing will be lost in translation. Even the media dullards will be able to figure out what's going on.   We are mad as hell and we'll not going to take it anymore.   This is our China Syndrome.   Our charge of the Light Brigade.   We invite our freedom loving friends from all over the world like Spain, France and the Dutch Netherland, who fought with us in our first Revolutionary war.   If there be any real men left, come join us.   We will loan you protest signs when you get here.   Obama has put your lively hoods and freedoms in jeopardy too.   By cozying up to China, North Korea, Russia, Cuba, and Iran the western world's freedom are on the trading block.   No longer do we let optimism rule the day.   Now we put our fear to our feet and march as one against the tyrants in Washington D.C. and in state capitals and city halls.   Freedom is not a "natural Occurrence" it must be soaked in the blood of patriots and tyrants.   We must demonstrate that we are not harmless innocent fetuses to be ripped out of our mother's womb and tossed into a trash can out back by these tyrants.   We want go quietly into the night. You want tread on us no more.   You no longer decide our fate in smoke filled rooms.   We are not bargaining chips that you discard in the pile.   We will demand the resignation of every godless liberal Democrat, and every gutless moderate Republican, regardless of the office or judgeship they hold.   Do yourself a favor and leave before we get there.   You don't want to see the white of our eyes. You have made it what it is, now can you handle it?   The tide has changed; the pendulum has swung.   Entrenched beaurocrats its time to find another line of work especially you in the State Department.   There will be no more stare decisus, no more done deal with the Supreme Court.   No longer will school prayer be illegal and infanticide abortion legal.   You Supreme Courts judge have ran foul of the law long enough. Since the congress want exercise its' "exceptions" clause duties, we will.   We will put a nativity scene in front of every city hall and state house.   You will teach our children reading, writing, arithmetic, and creationism not Heather has two moms and outcome base education.   2 + 2 is once again 4.   We ask no permission. We will overwhelm you with our sheer numbers.   The snail darter or any other made up endangered species no longer take precedence over our lives and our businesses.   We govern our own affairs.   We decide every abled body man works. No longer will the welfare state destroy Black families.   We will no longer shop at retailers too cowardly or politically correct to say Merry Christmas, starting with Wal-Mart. We will see how many Muslims, Orthodox Jews, atheist and Buddhist buy Christmas gifts at your stores. Since you don't want to offend them, you have offended and disrespected the hell out of us long enough. So we sit the next "holiday season" out and open gifts left over from the last one. Today we hit the reset button. We are the roaring engine that drives things now. Feel our roar. We stand ready to stop bullets with our chest and not our backs. There's no surrender there will be no retreat. We honor our God and our families; our country, with our willingness to die for all. Sic Semper evello mortem tyrannis. To quote a realer president than the one we have, Thomas J. Whitmore "we will not go quietly into the night" and to quote one of the best presidents ever, Ronald Wilson Reagan, "we outlaw communism forever, we start bombing in five minutes." In the words of that great patriot on that fateful day Todd Beamer, "LET'S ROLL!" I thank you all. "PASS IT ON!"

www.ingramcontent.com/pod-product-compliance
Lightning Source LLC
Chambersburg PA
CBHW070137290526
45789CB00002B/522